Hippie Voices to God's Heart

Hippie Voices to God's Heart

Calvary Chapel Encounters God

DAVID L. REAM

Edited by John S. Knox

Foreword by Vernon M. Whaley

Afterword by Holland Davis

To Nick and Celeste
If we live in the Spirit
Let us walk in the Spirit. Gal 5:25

God Bless,
DAViD Ream

WIPF & STOCK · Eugene, Oregon

HIPPIE VOICES TO GOD'S HEART
Calvary Chapel Encounters God

Wipf & Stock
An Imprint of Wipf and Stock Publishers
199 W. 8th Ave., Suite 3
Eugene, OR 97401

www.wipfandstock.com

PAPERBACK ISBN: 978-1-6667-7988-2
HARDCOVER ISBN: 978-1-6667-7989-9
EBOOK ISBN: 978-1-6667-7990-5

01/22/24

To the people I love, who teach me
more of God's love through their own—
Jesus Christ, Sharon my wife, my sons, my family,
and the saints of God.

"And we have known and believed the love
that God hath to us.
God is love; and he that dwelleth in love dwelleth in God,
and God in him (1 John 4:16 KJV).

Contents

Foreword

"Great Awakenings" are times of spiritual renewal when the Holy Spirit prompts the confession of sin by God's people. These God-encounters are world-wide in scope. The body of Christ has experienced revival and awakenings of great magnitude, consequence, and influence at various times in history. Scholars and church historians call these spiritual encounters times of awakening because of the magnitude of spiritual influence they have on culture, the church, and individuals.

Worship is at the heart of every great awakening and movement of God. They always include recommitment to God, repentance of sin, and believers living in personal holiness. There is usually some type of recommitment to social ministries (feeding the poor, reaching out to the homeless, including the marginalized, and so on) and change in culture. In general, God brings people back to himself.

With each great awakening or revival comes a renewed commitment to worship, conviction of sin, and awareness of God's holiness. Interestingly, every great awakening is influenced by college age students (17–22 years of age). Culturally, nearly every great awakening has been met with serious criticism from within "the church," no matter the denominational affiliation, and surrounding culture. Historically, changes in music, worship styles, and open expressions of emotion accompany every great awakening. They are often characterized by personal evangelism and a sense of urgency to tell others about Christ.

For certain, the Jesus movement was part of a revival that swept across America and circled the globe in the late 1960s and early 1970s. Many of the early "Jesus People"—as they were called by the mainstream media—were former hippies that turned to Christianity and away from drug addiction, occult influences, Eastern religions and mysticism, and atheism. These "Jesus people" embraced Christ as savior but did not abandon aspects of their sub-culture, including informal dress, rock music, casual speech, and simple living. While they rejected the sins of hippies, they adapted some aspects of the counterculture to a Christian context. For instance, they lived in communes but rejected sexual immorality.

One ministry that had a notable impact on hippies and the Jesus movement was Calvary Chapel in Costa Mesa, California. On one occasion, Chuck Smith, the pastor of Calvary Chapel, took his wife out for coffee on the Palisades overlooking Huntington Beach in Southern California. Stretched out on the beach for miles in each direction were baby boomers, soaking in the sun, and enjoying the water. Smith's wife, Kay, said to him, "Why don't you go down there and preach Jesus to them?" He replied, "You don't do that," and promptly forgot about her suggestion—until later that night, when during prayer, Smith said he heard the Holy Spirit say to him, "Why don't you go down there and preach Jesus to them?" Again, he put it out of his head.

The next morning, he felt the Holy Spirit's prompting again. So, that afternoon, he took off his suit, tie, and white shirt and donned a golf shirt, khakis, and tennis shoes. He took a Bible to the beach and began to preach Jesus. After about an hour, one of the young people said, "Here is water. Can we be baptized?" Smith took off his shoes, waded into the Pacific Ocean, and began baptizing young people. Youth from all over the beach began running to see the "religious experience."

With an even larger crowd later that same day, Smith began preaching Jesus again. More than two hundred young people confessed Jesus Christ as Lord and were baptized. The next day, the same thing happened. Smith preached on the beach and again hundreds received Christ and were baptized in the Pacific Ocean. Smith invited them to his church in Costa Mesa, and on Sunday morning, the "Jesus people" showed up.

These new Christians—men with long hair and jeans, women in unapologetically simple attire—seemed out of place among the traditional Pentecostal audience of smartly dressed Christians. Yet, the new Jesus people congregation grew. They moved into a rented Lutheran church facility and later into an abandoned school. Next, they moved to an eleven-acre plot of undeveloped land, and then built an auditorium there that seated 2,200.[1]

Their worship services were unique. Worshipers sang newly composed songs for three and four hours, prayed, and devoted themselves to serious Bible study. It was a movement built on biblical, verse-by-verse, expositional preaching. Smith's preaching was well suited for the Jesus people. He started at Genesis 1:1 and preached chapter-by-chapter through the King James Bible—Sunday mornings, Sunday evenings, and Wednesday evenings. When he finished Revelation 22:21 some years later, he began again in Genesis 1:1.

At one point, the church was winning more than two hundred to Christ each week, and in a normal month approximately nine hundred were baptized in the Pacific Ocean. On one occasion, more than 3,000 came to watch a baptism, after which Smith presented the gospel and saw even more come to Christ. Smith's congregation grew to fill four separate preaching services each weekend and became one of the largest churches in America. When Smith's disciples had built churches, they typically built mega-churches. Smith's church spawned other similar congregations, and the Calvary Chapel phenomenon became a movement.

The Jesus movement lasted a little more than a decade, but in that time, its effect on evangelicalism was momentous. During the years that followed, thousands of Jesus movement converts assumed leadership in local churches, para-church organizations, and denominations. All the Calvary Chapel churches, Hope Chapel churches, Horizon Christian Ministries, Vineyard churches,

---

1. Towns and Whaley, *Worship Through the Ages*, 296–302.

and Jews for Jesus trace their roots to the Jesus movement. These church groups developed into large, influential associations with hundreds of congregations around the globe. Their combined membership exceeds one million.

A multi-million-dollar contemporary Christian music industry—with global influences, implication, inspiration, and impact—was birthed by the Jesus movement. Thousands of congregations secured full-time youth pastors to manage and nurture their growing youth populations. According to historian Robb Redman, the Jesus movement preserved "the substance of Christian worship . . . in a new format, especially in their emphasis on biblical preaching, prayer, and congregational participation."[2]

In this book, David L. Ream presents "a deep-dive" scholarly treatise on the role that one pastor at one church can have on the larger, world-wide evangelical movement. The testimony of a pastor and church defines a ministry—a legacy—deeply committed to teaching the word of God to a generation in desperate need of a divine touch from the throne of God. Ream carefully blends an evaluation of the theological, biblical, cultural, and doctrinal influences that the Holy Spirit used to prepare Chuck Smith, Calvary Chapel, and their continuing influence on the body of Christ nearly sixty years after the revival began. The stories and issues surrounding the Jesus movement and Calvary Chapel highlight a deeper working of the Holy Spirit still at work in the church of Jesus Christ today.

The reality that God may once again make his presence and glory known to this present generation prompts historians, teachers of worship, and lovers of Jesus to ask many questions: "Is there another Great Awakening on the horizon (?); will there be another Jesus movement (?); is God placing his hand of anointing and blessing on other congregations like Calvary Chapel (?); is God raising up yet another Holy Spirit filled personality to lead this generation into a new, heaven-sent awakening (?); if the next awakening is like those from the past, will it introduce to the church—along with

2. Redman, *Great Worship Awakening*, 54.

God's overwhelming presence—major paradigm shifts in the way evangelicals worship during the twenty-first century?"

Culturally secular, political writer for *The Atlantic Monthly*, *The New York Times*, and *The Los Angeles Times*, Lauren Sandler suggests, "We are poised before the next Great Awakening in American History."[3] If this is the case, one would expect to see significant "road signs" as God ushers in the next awakening. I would suggest the following ten indicators of a worship renewal on the horizon of the same magnitude that Calvary Chapel experienced during the late 1960s:

1. Worship is at the heart to every Great Awakening and movement by God.

2. There is always a recommitment to God, repentance from sin, and change in personal behavior toward holiness and righteousness.

3. There is often a rediscovery within the body of Christ to obeying the biblical mandate for meeting social needs (feeding the poor, reaching out to the marginalized, and so on).

4. God always provides opportunity for people to understand and communicate worship in their own vernacular and culture.

5. God always uses people to proclaim His wonders. Moreover, it is imperative to keep in perspective that all the great awakenings experienced by the evangelical community included a generation of highly energized young, college-aged students.

6. God is in the business of changing people and worship of him as sovereign is at the heart of this change.

7. Prepare for it. Any new awakening will be met with serious criticism from within the established church and the surrounding culture.

8. Since 2000, worship practices and new paradigms have been influenced by the introduction of technology into

---

3. Sandler, *Righteous*, 11.

congregational worship services, with greater emphasis on smaller groups, praise teams, worship choir, integration of lighting, sound, and so on.

9. In general, there is a greater connection (through various forms of communication, social media, internet technology, etc.) between the church and the mainstream community.

10. Most of us believe God uses times of great awakenings to make his glory known, draw people unto himself, and unify his people—the church. In the process, culture is changed, marriages are restored, thousands turn from sin, and people's lives are forever transformed.

While the secular humanist may be threatened by the sheer notion that another great awakening is imminent, those of us that worship Jesus Christ take great courage in knowing "God's Story" continues. What liberalism calls anti-intellectual, backward, and "rear-view mentality" is (in reality) a working of the Holy Spirit. Sandler is correct when she says, "An awakening entails young people,"[4] because it takes a youth movement to reach critical mass.

God is moving in a mighty way, drawing this next generation—the Disciple Generation[5]—to himself and he is doing this through the worship of Jesus. As we make inquiry into the next great awakening (perhaps even seeing God raise up yet another influential pastor/congregation team like Smith's), let us keep our eyes looking to the "author and finisher of our faith" (Heb 12:2)—Jesus, the source for all Holy Spirit-led revival.

Vernon M. Whaley, DMin, DWS, PhD
Associate Provost and Dean
School of Music and Worship Arts, Trevecca Nazarene University
Founding Dean of the School of Music, Liberty University (2005–2020)

4. Sandler, *Righteous*, 12.
5. Sandler, *Righteous*, 5.

Preface

I was convicted. A verse of scripture halted my studies while reading problem-solution research in the field of Christian Worship. The method I had been reading follows this pattern: Find (or worse *create*) a problem with someone's worship ministry. Diagnose the problem. Then propose a solution to resolve the problem and improve the future of worship. The verse that came to mind was, "Who are you to pass judgment on another's servant? Before his own master he stands or falls. And he will stand, for the Lord is able to make him stand" (Rom 14:4 NET). It convinced me this method is inappropriate for this field. Taken to task by what came to mind as imperative, I knew I was led to determine a different approach from what I had been reading.

The conviction for me was that this problem solution method deserves the same rebuke as the Disciples critical of Mary who anointed Jesus before His crucifixion. He told them flatly, "Let her alone" (John 12:7). For me, there could be no criticizing of another's Christian worship. I reasoned that when a worship leader is prayerfully serving their congregation, and the Lord is being worshipped in Spirit and in Truth, I greatly err to critique that ministry.

I was to discover superlative and exemplary situations. New Testament worship permits latitude since there is only a scintilla of prescriptive material to guide a church. In God's foreknowledge, this latitude appears necessary as Christianity continues globally "Until the full number of the Gentiles has come in" (Rom 11:25). Is there a group of Christian worshippers who are among the largest and fastest growing, who honor the Word of God in their worship, and where the Holy Spirit works through them to duplicate successful patterns of ministry? My aim was to isolate biblical, transcendent, repeatable characteristics for application as God intended.

What follows is what I found. I pray it assists you as you participate in Christian Worship—the business of heaven on earth.

Acknowledgments

Love constrains me to acknowledge those who have a direct hand in this book. First is God. Without God nothing is possible, and with God all things are possible (Mark 10:27).

Sharon, my wife, thank you for being a woman of tremendous godly vision who saw this when I did not. Your confidence in me exceeds my expectations of myself. Without your belief, encouragement, and support I never would have thought to do this. You prove what the love of God accomplishes. I am grateful to God for bringing us together as a witness of His love for all.

To our sons, Aaron and Jacob, your inquiries on my progress and well-wishing along the way kept me on track.

Dr. Vernon Whaley, your words have always been a source of encouragement and a trustworthy beacon pointing the way forward. Every interaction with you has edified me. Drs. Connell and Rumrill, thank you for your support at Liberty University and for trusting the process to guide me. Dr. John S. Knox, my editor, for placing my work for acceptance within academia and nurturing my voice. Pastor Holland Davis (the real PHD) for continuing in the Holy Scriptures and the Holy Spirit, serving true worshippers, and for recognizing this book's value. For those who walk with the Lord, there still is "MORE!" As Pastor Chuck Smith said, "Everything is preparation for something else."

Finally, I acknowledge present and future worshippers whom I have never met. You are partakers of a heavenly calling and God has planted you as the desire of my heart (Ps 37:4). He quickened His calling in me through Ephesians 2:1–10 and Psalm 145. I pray

Acknowledgments

for your faithful service in love as we consider the faithful example of the apostle and high priest Jesus Christ, our Lord and Savior (Heb 3:1–6).

1

Countercultural, Not American Idolatry Culture

THE LEAD PASTOR AND worship leader roles have changed since the mid-twentieth century. Although God (Mal 3:6)[1] and the Gospel (1 Cor 15:1–7) do not change, the challenges presented by culture do, and the church's interaction with culture necessitates style changes. Lead pastors leverage specialized music ministers to maximize their strengths and reduce the burdens on any single person to accommodate increasingly complex technological demands. The correlated worship leader role expands and increases the missional capacity of worship as music impacts the worship ministry and culture. Aniol mentions, "The most missional worship is that which seeks to glorify God in making disciple-worshipers by communicating God's truth through the use of appropriate cultural forms that are regulated by Scripture."[2]

The worshipping church continues Jesus' aim of the Great Commission—making worshipping disciples and maturing

1. Nearly all biblical passages referenced in this work employ the *King James Version*, published in 1769, public domain. The KJV Bible is the book that Chuck Smith's mother used as she taught him how to read. His Scripture memorization, the preaching he heard, the teaching at the Bible school that he attended, and his preaching were based on this ubiquitous version.

2. Aniol, *Waters of Babylon*, 117.

believers in Christ. This book examines a historically significant local church, Calvary Chapel Costa Mesa (CCCM) that continues to influence culture today. It became a megachurch, spawned a megachurch movement, and birthed the musical genre of Contemporary Christian Music.

The global impact of the Jesus movement continues through Calvary Chapel with its simplicity and its biblical mission of teaching the word of God—balanced with experiential aspects of living a spiritually transformed life by and for Jesus Christ. The body of Christ remains faithful to the unchangeable truth of Scripture while ministering to the saints to bear the fruit of the Gospel, the fruit of the Spirit, and its original mission.

CCCM has Pentecostal roots, but through Smith's submission to and application of the Bible, it has moderated Pentecostal stylings (being missional and scriptural) and caught the wave of the Holy Spirit, awakening a bevy of new believers and reviving those previously born again—not in idolatry but as an overflow of the Holy Spirit.

1.1 WHY CALVARY CHAPEL COSTA MESA?

Before the turn of the millennium, Donald E. Miller writes in *Reinventing American Protestantism,* "Calvary Chapel can be viewed as the pioneer of new paradigm churches."[3] Miller correctly identifies CCCM as "the mother church"[4] of hundreds of churches across America that use the words, "Calvary Chapel," to name their church. CCCM presents a paradigmatic ministry style that has replicated around the world. Outsiders try to analyze and deconstruct, and yet, the insiders just smile and keep on abiding.

Outside observers during the Jesus movement that began in the late 1960s, caught a passing glimpse, much like Nicodemus did when he heard of the miracles in Galilee and saw the original Jesus movement in Jerusalem at the Passover (John 2:23). To

---

3. Miller, *Reinventing American Protestantism,* 37.

4. Miller, *Reinventing American Protestantism,* 35.

Nicodemus, Jesus explained, "The wind bloweth where it listeth, and thou hearest the sound thereof, but canst not tell whence it cometh, and whither it goeth: so is every one that is born of the Spirit" (John 3:8). There is life abundant in the Spirit of God, which defies thorough categorization for unredeemed people (1 Cor 2:14). Jesus availed himself to CCCM, which caught the wave of the Spirit and collaborated with the Spirit of Christ (Rom 8:9). Insider Greg Laurie explains, "What gave legs to the Jesus Movement as it happened in Southern California—specifically, in Orange County, and later in Riverside, Downey, West Covina, San Diego, and elsewhere—was its connection to local churches."[5]

Ed Stetzer, Executive Director of the Billy Graham Center for Evangelism, claims, "If you are in a contemporary church, engaging culture, and planting churches, you are, in a sense, a child of Calvary Chapel and of Chuck Smith."[6] Stetzer's comment suggests CCCM's influence is to thousands more churches in America and around the world. As a refinement and extension of the spiritual renewal movement that came out of the *First Wave of Pentecostalism*[7] after WWII, millions[8] have been influenced by what God has done through *Chuck* Smith.[9] Smith's daughter Cheryl Brodersen says that God was looking for someone who would not take the credit for what God wanted to do and someone who would continually point people back to Jesus.[10] Jesus continues to build His church and (since Acts 2) he looks for yielded vessels to cooperate with him.

Chuck Smith, the pastor of Calvary Chapel Costa Mesa, became responsible for all teaching at CCCM in November 1965.[11] Decades later, speaking to those called into one's God-given Christian ministry Smith states plainly: "To know success and

5. Laurie et al., *Jesus Revolution*, 49.

6. Stetzer, "Thoughts on the Amazing Life."

7. See Fig. 1 in chapter three for additional information.

8. "American Christianity Turning Charismatic?"

9. Guzik, "Remembering Pastor Chuck Smith," 46:07.

10. Peretski and Peretski, *What God Hath Wrought*, 24:42–25:06.

11. Fromm, "Textual Communities," 147.

effectiveness in our ministry, we must strive to be led by the Holy Spirit in everything we do. That is what the first-century church learned to do very early on."[12]

On revivalism Ed Hindson states, "There is no explanation except that a sovereign God works in the hearts of men by His Spirit, and that He dispenses His blessings whenever and wherever He chooses!"[13] In the twenty-first century, after the Jesus movement matured, Smith "established a 21-member leadership council to oversee the Calvary Church Association, a fellowship of some 1,600 like-minded congregations in the United States and abroad."[14]

Calvary Chapel Costa Mesa originated in 1961 as an independent church and positioned itself as a non-denominational church to distance itself from First Wave Pentecostalism before Smith's arrival. Founding pastor Floyd Nelson and his successor Smith, separate from the other, found their unique path by amicably "going independent" from the Foursquare denomination. Sixty years later, the name, "Calvary Chapel," functions for cultural Christianity as what a non-denominational church looks like. Paradoxically, CCCM functions as the denomination of the non-denominational. Those original, missional impulses to live guided by the Bible and a life in the Spirit came out of autonomy and a yearning to please God.

Church planters that have mimicked CCCM looking to duplicate a successful pattern of ministry are antithetical to the impulses that began CCCM. Every believer yearns to stand before Christ and hear, "Well done thou good and faithful servant: thou hast been faithful over a few things, I will make thee ruler over many things: enter into the joy of thy lord" (Matt 25:21, 23). Yet, when one serves to boost their own power—and at the whim of the public eye—thinking she/he has done the Lord's work, instead of hearing, "Well done," hears, "I never knew you: depart from me, ye that work iniquity" (Matt 7:23b). Jesus' teaching and commanding

12. Smith, *Living*, 60.

13. Hindson, *Glory in the Church*, 55.

14. "Chuck Smith, 86, Dies."

His disciples at the occasion of washing His disciples' feet demonstrates a wholesome desire to be good stewards and fruitful in ministry (John 13:1–20). Jesus sets the example to follow (John 13:34–35). Fruitful ministry comes from the freedom found by personally following the Holy Spirit and the Holy Scriptures—a more dynamic balance than static imitation.

This desire to serve and express the love of Christ through Christian service is central to Jesus' disciples; however, Jesus warns that those only dabbling in Christian service, appearing spiritual, ostensibly casting out devils, prophesying, and other wonderful works (Matt 7:21–23), may instead be cultivating iniquity—not the will of the Father. The thoughtful, devout follower of Jesus Christ wants to please the Lord, assured that his service honors the heavenly father and eternal king. The apostle Peter assures Christians that God has given them all that is needed for life and godliness, and believers are kept from being barren and unfruitful (2 Pet 1:3–12).

Currently, there are at least three distinct and separate strains from the "Mother Church;" each to some degree was influenced from Smith's model. First, Smith selected prominent men in the movement for the Calvary Chapel Association (CCA) to serve the 1,800 (and growing) global affiliates. According to CCA, "The Lord has wonderfully and gracefully placed His Hand on the churches and missions of Calvary Chapel around the world, resulting in over 1,800 associated ministries under the umbrella of the Calvary Chapel Association."[15]

After Smith's passing, CCCM launched the Calvary Global Network (CGN) with the desire to "take all the amazing things we've learned from our past and carry them forward into the future, partnering together with like-minded ministry leaders across the globe in our mission."[16] Finally, there are local congregations founded by Smith's direct sons of the faith who established churches completely independent of either organization. One such independent founder is John Higgins who began, "With a sincere

15. "Calvary Chapel Association."
16. "About CGN."

concern for the lost, John, being used of the Lord had a burden for the generation of hippies and surfers, and was used in the Jesus movement of the Holy Spirit that spread from the West Coast to the East Coast, bringing thousands of young people to Jesus Christ back in the 60's."[17]

Presently, one of Higgins' ministries continues as His Church, Calvary Tri City, in Tempe, Arizona, which is "a fellowship of believers that study the Bible 'word by word' in order to edify, uplift and encourage each other. All those who wish to learn more about the Jesus Christ's Life and Ministry are welcome."[18]

1.2 CALVARY CHAPEL REPRESENTS FRUITFUL MINISTRY

Jesus' teachings are the basis of fruitful ministry. This pattern of ministry is worthy of consideration for church planters and builders who engage culture—to do the Lord's work in the Lord's way. Jesus taught that a tree is known by its fruit (Luke 6:44). Jesus extends the analogy of fruitfulness in John 15:16—"Ye have not chosen me, but I have chosen you, and ordained you, that ye should go and bring forth fruit, and that your fruit should remain: that whatsoever ye shall ask of the Father in my name, he may give it you." Smith and CCCM yielded to Jesus Christ as the head of the Church (Col 1:18; Eph 5:23) and led others by following the word of God and the Holy Spirit, showing the reality of the gospel of Christ.

Carrying the fruit analogy forward, the ability to reproduce is a biological hallmark of maturation. CCCM reproduced as it spawned a megachurch growth movement in the U.S. and with hundreds of churches of assorted sizes around the world. Judging by its fruit, the model exemplifies what Scott Aniol asserts as God's mission for the church: "Corporate worship accomplishes the mission of God by being what it is—worship; the most missional worship is that which acts out the gospel and communicates

---

17. His Church, "About."
18. His Church, "About."

God's truth using forms that are regulated by the authority of the Word of God."[19]

This book asserts that Calvary Chapel Costa Mesa distanced itself from the *First Wave of Pentecostalism* consonant with post-World War II impulses of the second wave but remained distinct from the second wave. As their fruitful ministry multiplied, they held their unique and influential position while remaining separate from the third and fourth waves. Its epistemological foundation is the Bible. Its metaphysical foundation is the active ministry of the Holy Spirit.

The movement most closely aligns with the *Second Wave of Pentecostalism* wherein God built his church according to Scripture. The church is God's idea—not a human idea. God communes spiritually with people who worship in spirit and in truth through the finished work of Jesus. God commissions the body of Christ to evangelize. The fruit is new congregations of Christians who worship in spirit and in truth. A congregation matures and reproduces by staying grounded in the word of God and living their faith in the power of the Holy Spirit.

Charismatic expressions of *Third and Fourth Waves of Pentecostalism* coincide with aspects of fruitful ministry found in the second wave of spiritual renewal but vary on the foundational position of Scripture to moderate the work of the Spirit. John Wimber, for example, as the self-styled founder of the *Third Wave of Pentecostalism*, "Opposed the idea that rank-and-file believers should abdicate their influence and ministry to a small group of spiritual superstars. He strongly believed that all believers have the gifts and abilities to influence others but that they need to be equipped to do it."[20]

Wimber fostered congregational reliance on a human leader to equip the saints. Smith would agree that equipping is needed (Eph 4:10–16); however, Jesus said He would build His church (Matt 16:18). Thus, the ultimate equipper of the saints is the word of God and the Spirit of Christ. These subtle variations—at the

19. Aniol, *Waters of Babylon*, 121.

20. Wimber and Springer, *Power Evangelism*, 182.

foundational level—lead second and third wave congregations in diverging directions.

The prototypical third wave assembly Hillsong was founded in 1983 and "transformed into a global assembly with over 100,000 adherents in 15 countries on five continents of the world. Its concomitant growth and influence upon global evangelical Christianity can be linked to a bewildering array of activities . . . Hillsong has proven adept at navigating."[21]

In many ways, they have pioneered a virtual church model, but is it what God has in mind for the twenty-first century? The theme of human effort bringing the kingdom of God to earth now is a position held by New Apostolic Reformation churches (NAR). As Eckhardt remarks, "Apostolic churches and networks are developing around the world as God is positioning His Church to fulfill the Great Commission. C. Peter Wagner calls this movement a 'new apostolic reformation.' It is a movement that ultimately will affect everyone within the Church."[22] The fundamental issue with this movement is that Jesus taught his disciples, "When ye pray, say, Our Father which art in heaven, Hallowed be thy name. Thy kingdom come. Thy will be done, as in heaven, so in earth" (Luke 11:2). NAR churches espouse a kingdom now coming through human effort, rather than allowing Christ to bring the Kingdom of God at His return.

Similarly, Independent Network Christianity churches (INC), express aspects of the Acts 2 church and thus, "Fall under the category of neo-Charismatic but differ in important ways from new paradigm churches: 1) They do not seek to build a 'movement' 2) They are not primarily focused on building congregations 3) They seek to transform society as a whole, and 4) are highly connected networks of cooperation."[23] Calvary Chapel's eschatological sensitivities seek Jesus to do the work of transforming of society in the way that the Lord wills.

---

21. Riches and Wagner, *Hillsong Movement*, 2.

22. Eckhardt, *Moving in the Apostolic*, 57.

23. Christerson, and Flory, *Network Christianity*, 8.

The *Third and Fourth waves of Pentecostalism* appear in media as stereotypical examples of Pentecostal expressions and impulses that belies their place in history. Paul Hawkes, critical of these examples, contrasts the Calvary Chapel model, which allows "churches to develop their own mission program, educate their own pastors, plant daughter churches. The arrangement is very loose."[24] This broader perspective comes not from media portrayals of Pentecostalism, but from a consistent literal, grammatical, historical interpretation of Scripture that emphasizes the way of the original church in the book of Acts.

Pentecostalism, in its broadest, *Renewalist* sense, is "one of (if not the) fastest-growing religious movements in the twentieth century—a movement found in every country of the world."[25] This fact tends to multiply God's glory and human fallibility. Globally, twenty-first-century Pentecostalism continues as Jesus directed in the Great Commission (Matt 28:16–20), and Calvary Chapel is part of that commission, attaining global influence. CCCM ministry replicates in ways received by those seeking to engage their culture and encounter God. By attending to the leading of the Holy Spirit and the teaching of Scripture, God has positioned CCCM as a paradigmatic church—a living object lesson for other renewalist movements.

Renewalists—in the broadest sense in Christianity—have critics, but the question that each generation needs to answer persists: Is a life untethered from Scripture what Jesus had in mind for His church? Lori Jensen notes, "There are many forms of Pentecostalism . . . when elements of Pentecostal worship (like speaking in tongues and animated worship) were borrowed and 'domesticated' by non-Pentecostal churches. The result looks like what takes place in Calvary Chapels."[26] However, life in the Spirit is more than speaking in tongues and hand waving.

Born-again believers of all Christian stripes may choose to "live as Jesus did, in his power and with his presence, seekers will

24. Hawkes, "Critical Analysis," 196.

25. Miller et al., *Spirit and Power*, 292.

26. Jensen, "(Re)Discovering Fundamentalism," 192.

be drawn . . . sharing Jesus will become a true delight and evangelism will become a lifestyle."[27] CCCM is not identical with but is most accurately understood as a second wave Pentecostal expression within the *Spiritual Renewal Movement*. Pastor Chuck and his wife Kay came of age in the *First Wave of Pentecostalism* during WWII but should not be conflated with the third or the fourth Wave Movements.

1.3 CALVARY CHAPEL'S PENTECOSTAL SITUATION

CCCM began just months after JFK became the first Catholic President of the United States in the 1960s—an age of hope mixed with trepidation over humanity's new opportunities. Many people felt that Kennedy's "Camelot" leadership would finally usher in a true brotherhood of mankind, "wherein each individual has reached the condition of a true brother to all mankind."[28] Somehow this would, in turn, bring the world to an idyllic panacea for prosperity and well-being.

This Utopianist ideal was shattered by the era's geo-political realities. Somewhere between the Cuban Missile Crisis and the Berlin Wall, the social forces behind the social movement were found wanting, suggesting, "A Hard Rain's A Gonna Fall."[29] The folkies, beatniks, and the earliest hippies were wary of the dead end for continuing materialism and unending avarice without love and peace. Many Protestants in the United States were eschatologically concerned that Pope John XXIII, Vatican II, and a Catholic President in the White House were a looming confluence embodying the antichrist. Was the United States headed in a worse direction—spiritually and socially?

Sharon Gardner Fisher attended the very first meeting of what would become CCCM with her husband, Hal, and their infant daughter. Fischer notes on CCCM's Pentecostal roots: "Hal

---

27. Pippert, *Out of the Saltshaker*, 87.

28. Farlow, "Brotherhood of Man."

29. Dylan, *The FreeWheelin' Bob Dylan*.

and I had come from Pentecostal backgrounds, and we were trying to find a church where we could feel at home. Joining up with a pastor with a similar background seemed like a good start."[30] The gathering did not have a name and began in a recreation center within a senior citizens' trailer park. Pastor Floyd Nelson gave a sermon, and his wife, Lois, led *a cappella* singing[31]—the first ministry team of CCCM.

Gardener also lists the first attendees of what would become CCCM: the elderly Maude Farrell and her friends (Golda Barnes, Hazel Cruncleton, Mrs. McClean, and Iva and Elisha Newman). Gardner previously knew the Nelsons and "had known Maude as a teenager when I attended the local Foursquare Church."[32] The Gardner's were the only young family in attendance.

Earlier, the Foursquare denomination, founded by Aimee Semple McPherson, was one of the major denominations formed out of the *First Wave of Pentecostalism*. Foursquare spread its influence in the early twentieth century and remains active in worldwide evangelism efforts. In 1923, "Sister Aimee" founded the Echo Park Evangelistic and Missionary Training Institute, consistent in obedience to the Great Commission and evangelistic impulses. English and Olena note, "The first class enrolled thirty-one men and sixty-eight women."[33] In 1926, it became LIFE Bible College. L.I.F.E. is an acronym for "Lighthouse of International Foursquare Evangelism." Both Chuck and Kay Smith trained for ministry at LIFE Bible college.[34]

The Nelsons left the Foursquare denomination independent of the Smiths. Both men were spiritual entrepreneurs seeking guidance from the Holy Spirit rather than a centrally controlled denominational system. In America, especially at that time, labeling a church as "Independent" was liberating, allowing one to

30. Fischer, *I Remember*, 23.

31. Fischer, *I Remember*, 23. "Cruncleton" as Fischer spells it and "Krunkelton" as Fromm records it.

32. Fischer, *I Remember*, 22–23.

33. English and Olena, *Women in Pentecostal*, 18.

34. Miller et al., *Spirit and Power*, 236.

follow one's own conscience by following the Lord, led by the holy Scriptures and the Holy Spirit.

The pastor's wife, Lois, had come up with the name for their gathering.[35] Fischer felt the name, *Calvary Chapel*, promoted respectability, was non-denominational, and not associated with classical Pentecostal nomenclature.[36] This strategic positioning is consistent with first wave impulses for a wider acceptance among mainline evangelicals and for outreach to the unsaved that manifested after WW II in the *Second Wave of Pentecostalism*.

The Foursquare denomination's influence is noteworthy to Calvary Chapel on at least two points. First is the direct connection with an original denomination coming out of classical Pentecostalism of the early twentieth century.[37] Second is the influence of women in twentieth and twenty-first-century ministries. Fromm observes: "The Pastor's wife is often seen as a strong partner and even a co-equal in pastoral authority and responsibility."[38] Nelson's wife, active in platform leadership of the congregational worship service, set much of what characterizes the Pentecostal tone of the fellowship.

Charles E. Fromm's seminal work, "Textual Communities and New Song in the Multimedia Age: The Routinization of Charisma in the Jesus Movement,"[39] is a case study of CCCM. The original board members were "basically white middle-class conservative Orange-Countians including an engineer, architect, police sergeant, real estate developer, a gas station owner, and fashion model."[40] After three meetings, the senior center denied Sunday-to-Sunday meetings to the fledgling group each week, so they relocated to a nearby Girl Scout meeting hall and settled there in 1962.[41]

35. Fromm, "Textual Communities," 136.

36. Fischer, *I Remember*, 25.

37. Towns and Whaley, *Worship Through Ages*, 229, 381.

38. Fromm, "Textual Communities," 137–38.

39. Fromm, "Textual Communities," ii.

40. Fromm, "Textual Communities," 136.

41. Fischer, *I Remember*, 26.

The Smiths trained and served in the Foursquare denomination for seventeen years before becoming independent. Thus, a direct tie to the *First Wave of Pentecostalism* can be established. As the pastor's wife, Kay was not as prominent as Lois Nelson, but she served as a pianist and in various leadership capacities for years at CCCM.[42]

42. Fischer, *I Remember*, 60.

2

Two Essential Indicators of Pentecostalism

CLARIFYING THE ORIGINS OF twentieth-century Pentecostalism situates Calvary Chapel within the body of Christ and reveals its parallels with the *Second Wave of Pentecostalism*. Pentecostalism is an umbrella term that stems from the Israelites' commemoration of Pentecost as described in Acts 2 signifying the birthday of the New Testament church. The apostle Luke documents the spread of the Holy Spirit beginning in Jerusalem at the temple on Pentecost, through "All Judaea, and in Samaria, and unto the uttermost part of the earth" (Acts 1:8).

Modern-day Pentecostalism challenges precise definition because it lacks uniform expression and is multifaceted with some twenty-three thousand denominations worldwide.[1] Since God's Spirit flows through his people, a multiplicity of expressions is not surprising. However, as one defines Pentecostalism, the definition can become a delimitation as one tends to see that for which one looks. One Pentecostal theologian, Yong, sidestepped the issue, avoiding a definition asserting, "Pentecostalism broadly will emerge over the course of this volume."[2]

---

1. Espinosa, *William J. Seymour*, 1.
2. Yong, *Spirit Poured Out*, 19.

Gastón Espinoza provides additional clarity with two essential Pentecostal characteristics despite what at first appears to be numerous distinctions and contrasting definitions: "The first is the necessity of having a personal, born-again conversion experience with Jesus Christ, and the second is a desire to be baptized and filled with the Holy Spirit—or being born-again and Spirit-filled."[3] He notes, "Contrary to stereotypes, a person does not have to speak in tongues to be considered a Pentecostal or Charismatic Christian, but they normally desire to do so."[4]

2.1 THE BORN-AGAIN EXPERIENCE

The born-again experience stems from Jesus' comments to Nicodemus in John 3 and his explicit command at verse 7: "Ye must be born again." This is reiterated in 1 Peter 1:3 ("begotten again") and 1 Peter 1:23 ("Being born again"). Espinoza's distinctive points agree with CCCM and are foundational to the teaching of pastor Chuck Smith.

Smith taught that the Holy Spirit's primary workings are represented in the Greek biblical text by three prepositions: *para, en,* and *epi.*

Para is often translated as "with" and *en* translated as "in." Both are found in John 14:15–18 and are emphasized by italics in Jesus' context.

> If ye love me, keep my commandments. And I will pray the Father, and he shall give you another Comforter, that he may abide with you forever; Even the Spirit of truth; whom the world cannot receive, because it seeth him not, neither knoweth him: but ye know him; for he dwelleth *with* you, and shall be *in* you. I will not leave you comfortless: I will come to you.

3. Espinosa, *William J. Seymour,* 1.
4. Espinosa, *William J. Seymour,* 1.

The *en* experience, subsequent to *para,* is the initial indwelling of the Holy Spirit. Both of which are distinct from the *epi* or overflow of the Comforter—also known as the Holy Spirit.

The *para* experience is first. Jesus describes the Holy Spirit's ubiquitous work among all humanity in John 16:7–15 and leads the recipient to become born-again. The Spirit dwells in the justified, sanctified believer in the completed work of Jesus as Savior. Being born-again necessitates the Holy Spirit's work of baptizing the new convert into the body of Christ. As Paul writes, "For by one Spirit are we all baptized into one body, whether we be Jews or Gentiles, whether we be bond or free; and have been all made to drink into one Spirit" (1 Cor 12:13). A born-again experience is essential for leadership at Calvary Chapel.

Smith explains the background for a third spiritual experience—the *epi* experience—as not merely containing the Holy Spirit indwelling the believer, but by being constantly filled with the Holy Spirit to the overflowing. Smith states, "Thus, we believe that every born-again believing child of God has the Holy Spirit dwelling in him. He is under the injunction of the scriptures to yield his body to the control of the Holy Spirit and to be constantly filled with the Holy Spirit."[5]

The *epi* experience may immediately follow the indwelling so closely that it may be experienced as a singular event, as shown in Acts 10:44–48. The distinctive feature of being filled to the overflow by the Holy Spirit is being biblically grounded[6] and manifests around the world in a plethora of biblical ways to "keep the unity of the Spirit in the bond of peace" (Eph 4:3).

2.2 THE EMPOWERMENT FOR SERVICE

Pastor Smith taught that the *epi* experience was the overflow of the Spirit of one's relationship with Christ:

---

5. Smith, *Calvary Chapel Distinctives,* 29.

6. Luke 4:18; John 1:32–33; Acts 1:8; 2:17–18.

We could argue over theological terms, but the experience is described as a gushing forth of torrents of Living Water from our innermost being. So whatever name you call it isn't important. The main question we must ask concerning this necessary empowering experience for the ministry is simple: DO YOU HAVE IT?[7]

Pentecostal historian Espinoza's documentation of these two features agrees with Smith's foundational teachings for becoming a believer and for maturing believers. These documented features place CCCM doctrinally well within a broad Pentecostal context.

2.2.1 Literal Interpretation of Scripture as a Pattern for Living

Smith's charismatic interpretive approach to scripture is characteristic of his teaching ministry. He sought to honor and uphold the literalness and authority of Scripture as the inspired word of God and to keep these truths open to all who hear God's call—while maintaining the unity of the Spirit within the body of Christ. He taught that divisiveness within the body of Christ was sin, and yet he also recognized that God, being resplendently infinite, could be worshipped and honored biblically in a multitude of ways. He interpreted the truth of Scripture without compromise and remained open to growing Christ's church God's way.[8] Smith ministered the Sunday service with born-again, Spirit-filled and Spirit-empowered servant-leaders.

People receptive to this ministry want to know Jesus biblically (and experientially) without over-analyzing what God is doing, just as a surfer primarily wants the experience of riding a good wave and learning as the need arises. Thus, by surfing, the surfer learns by experience what makes a good wave to catch. This practical desire for experience supplemental to scriptural and the Holy

7. Smith, *Calvary Chapel Distinctives*, 32.
8. Smith, *Word for Today Bible*, 1483.

Spirit knowledge can lead to an anti-intellectual characterization.[9] These Christians learn by living the Christian life, balancing scripture, and yielding to indwelling Holy Spirit.

2.2.2 Like the Baptists, Like Pentecostals Yet Distinct

The ironic anecdote is that Baptists see Calvary Chapel as Pentecostals, and Pentecostals see Calvary Chapel as Baptists.[10] People inside and outside of Calvary Chapel alternatively see Calvary Chapel as Pentecostal, not Pentecostal, or as a non-issue. Miller, in his landmark research on "New Paradigm Churches" for the twenty-first century, found that "Calvary Chapel fits somewhere in the broad spectrum between Baptists and Pentecostals."[11]

Smith, like Baptists, relies upon Bible teaching as "the central goal of worship."[12] As a Pentecostal, he believes in the gifts of the Spirit, but "They should never be the focus of worship."[13] Paraphrasing Chuck Smith's inclusiveness from another context, if believers are to be fishers of men, then they should fish in the biggest pond: "We don't take a typical Pentecostal view, nor do we take a typical Baptist view. The minute you set your position one way or the other, you've lost half of your congregation . . . Our desire is to be able to minister to as broad a group of people as possible."[14]

Present Pentecostal theology engages "the broad spectrum of academic conversations as a full dialog partner seeking to learn but also able to contribute something fresh"[15] to address a global community. Smith's intention, like Nelson before him, was to draw from the widest possible social context and remain open to who God would draw into His Kingdom through one's earthly ministry.

9. Nel, "Rather Spirit-Filled," 1–9.

10. MacIntosh and Reis, "Venture of Faith," 9:03–9:10.

11. Miller, *Reinventing American Protestantism,* 36.

12. Miller, *Reinventing American Protestantism,* 36.

13. Miller, *Reinventing American Protestantism,* 36.

14. Smith, *Calvary Chapel Distinctives,* 107.

15. Yong, *Spirit Poured Out,* 30.

This balanced perspective combining the objective truth of the Bible with the subjective experience of the Holy Spirit opened a door of consciousness for the hippies. Their desire for all that God has for the born-again believer connected with their spiritual hunger for objective and subjective truth. Knowledge—intellectual and experiential—was available through the gifts of the Holy Scripture and the active ministry of Holy Spirit. This present reality remains appealing as CCCM nestles within Pentecostalism coinciding with Espinosa's two essential characteristics. How Smith used scripture to moderate the gift of tongues in the church further situates CCCM in the *Second Wave of Pentecostalism* in the Body of Christ and provided a trustworthy social context, capable of embracing the hippies when they came.

2.2.3 Tongues at Calvary Chapel Costa Mesa

Speaking in tongues—*glossolalia*—is sometimes considered a lead indicator of, and often associated with, the Pentecostal faith.[16] However, as Espinosa has noted, the born-again experience and the overflow of the Spirit are the essentials of Pentecostal faith consonant with the second wave of charismatic renewal. Speaking in tongues is not the initial evidence of Pentecostal faith in the second wave. Espinoza confirms, "There are two types of tongues: a divinely given human language one has never studied (*xenolalia*—Acts 2) and a divinely given language known only to God (*glossolalia*—in all other accounts in Acts 8:17–19, 10:44–46, 19:1– 6)."[17]

Moreover, since *glossolalia* is unintelligible speech known only to God, it is possible to publicly speak gibberish to appear spiritually superior among sincere believers who do not speak in tongues and who will not artificially manifest a spiritual gift not given to them. Thus, in practice, the belief that Spirit baptism is evidenced by tongues can encourage fakery. CCCM guards against

16. Félix-Jäeger, *Renewal Worship*, 12.
17. Espinosa, *William J. Seymour*, 2.

abuses of counterfeit spiritual gifts.[18] Nonetheless, it would be remiss to associate the Pentecostal label with CCCM and not address the tongues phenomenon within CCCM.

Historically, tongues in Sunday morning services at CCCM presented an early leadership challenge that Smith met and, in retrospect, produced a lasting benefit for the worship life and the use of this supposed controversial gift.[19] Smith resolved this challenge with reliance on the inerrancy of Scripture to moderate the gift. Tongues, as a phenomenon, manifested on the church's birthday (Acts 2:6–12). On that day, Jesus' disciples waited and prayed (Acts 1:12–15) for the Holy Spirit to empower them to be Christ's witnesses (Acts 1:8). Jesus prophesied a "promise from the Father" (Acts 1:4) before the ascension and reception into heaven.

What is undeniable in the Acts 2 text is that this manifestation, adequately termed, is not *glossolalia* but *xenolalia*, "because that every man heard them speak in his own language" (Acts 2:6). The Galilean disciples spoke different languages/dialects. The crowd that assembled in Jerusalem at the feast day affirmed, "We do hear them speak in our tongues the wonderful works of God" (Acts 2:11). Smith, from the scriptures, understood that God had given the church everything it needed as it learned to depend upon him. However, as a shepherd of God's flock, Smith aligned orthodoxy and orthopraxy by rightly dividing the word of truth to guide practice. Fromm states that Pastor Smith believed *glossolalia* spontaneously occurring "demonstrates insensitivity to decorum and common sense ignoring the admonition of Paul."[20] Paul's admonition—"Let all things be done decently and in order" (1 Cor 14:40)—is taken in context to moderate the Spirit's gifts to the church.

Before the hippies arrived, Smith assumed the responsibilities as teaching pastor and song leader. He gently corrected and affirmed the congregation that prophecy and tongues are gifts for today (and

18. Gainey, *The Afterglow*, 19.
19. Balmer, *Mine Eyes Have Seen*, 27.
20. Fromm, "Textual Communities," 155.

only until Christ returns). They are to be desired but used decently and in order as summed up in 1 Corinthians 14:39–40.[21]

2.2.4 Inerrancy at Calvary Chapel Costa Mesa

Randall Balmer, in the twenty-fifth anniversary edition of his highly influential book, *Mine Eyes Have Seen The Glory*, presents the following view from a sociological perspective: "Chuck Smith clearly interprets scripture literally and in its plainest sense, with the presumption of inerrancy, but he is remarkably undogmatic by nature.[22] While Balmer ignores the *xenolalia-glossolalia* distinction as the Acts 2 narrative reports on the day of Pentecost, he accurately describes Smith's inerrant approach. He also raises the widespread issue of tongues in the charismatic movement within mainline denominations.

The gifts of the Spirit (aka, the *Charismata*) moderated within traditional denominations are characteristic of the *Second Wave of Pentecostalism*. Balmer continues: "Many Pentecostals (such as the Church of God or the Assemblies of God or the International Church of the Foursquare Gospel) regard this spiritual blessing as an essential mark of a true Christian."[23] Balmer also asserts, "Chuck Smith's latitudinarianism, his unwillingness to engage in theological battles that he views as irrelevant, has defused many of the controversies that afflict other evangelical churches."[24]

Emphasizing inerrancy, unwavering reliance on the biblical text, and teaching the whole counsel of God (Acts 20:27), Smith guided pastors and teachers:

> When you come to difficult issues that deal with problems in an individual's life or within the church body, you can address them straightforwardly . . . People in the congregation know that it's simply the passage of

---

21. Fromm, "Textual Communities," 155–56.
22. Balmer, Mine Eyes Have Seen, 26.
23. Balmer, *Mine Eyes Have Seen*, 26.
24. Balmer, *Mine Eyes Have Seen*, 27.

scripture being studied that day . . . one of the best commentaries on the Bible is the Bible itself.[25]

Therefore, resolving issues requires a whole counsel approach.

One germane example of how Smith used scripture to guide and moderate practice in the worship service is 1 Corinthians 14:3, of which, Smith notes, "Prophecy defined here is speaking 'edification, exhortation and comfort' to the people. That is what we do when we teach the Word. Speaking in tongues is self-edifying, which is good, but speaking prophetically edifies the whole body, and that is better in the assembly."[26] According to 1 Corinthians 14:3, prophesying is a spoken gift from God, and yet distinct from tongues.

Smith reasoned from the Scriptures that teaching is the appropriate gift for a public worship service, and the Holy Spirit would not be interrupting Himself with a personal gift.[27] According to Smith, "God's purpose for spiritual phenomena has never been to attract attention or to put on display, which unfortunately seems to be the case in many churches today. Whatever happens in our corporate gathering should be for the edification of all."[28] Therefore, teaching would have the priority in public meetings. Fromm agrees on the issue when he states, "The function of spiritual gifts for service and the ultimate nature of the *ecclesia* as a charismatic structure that creates community and is not for the benefit of the individual."[29]

This distinction of the Sunday morning service being a public meeting—and the traditional time a visitor might come to church—is central in the reasoning of Smith and would guide decisions regarding the worship service on Sunday mornings spanning his forty-eight-year tenure at CCCM. Smith maintained that the gift of tongues is "wonderful for someone to exercise in their

25. Smith, *Calvary Chapel Distinctives*, 53.

26. Smith, *Word for Today Bible*, 1498.

27. Gainey, *The Afterglow*, 12.

28. Smith, *Word for Today Bible*, 1499.

29. Fromm, "Textual Communities," 156.

private times of worship."[30] The Apostle Paul substantiates Smith's claim: "In the church, I had rather speak five words with my understanding, that by my voice I might teach others also, than ten thousand words in an unknown tongue" (1 Cor 14:18–19). Thus, spiritual gifts are evident at CCCM. Nevertheless, CCCM held Believer's Meetings or Afterglow Services—not public services—where tongues, interpretation of tongues, and prophecy were pursued in an intimate setting according to scripture.

2.3 GOD'S WORD EDIFYING IS IN, SELF-EXALTATION IS OUT

The gatherings on Sunday mornings at Calvary Chapel Costa Mesa were public meetings open to all people—including unbelievers, not-yet believers, and believers—who hopefully would encounter God through a purposeful worship service of musical praising, teaching, and prophesying, but also through leadership who aimed for the edification of all people regardless of their position in Christ. Drawing attention to oneself or exalting the human instrument submitted to God was not in the picture.

The Spirit of Christ was free to minister according to the will of God voiced in the inspired text. American idolatry and self-glorification were not permitted. The Sunday morning worship service was both similar to and yet distinct from mainline evangelicalism, and at the same time, it coincided with aspects of Pentecostalism— a unique position among twentieth-century Christian churches.

---

30. Smith, *Word for Today Bible*, 1498.

3

The Four Waves of Pentecostalism
and Calvary Chapel

RESEARCHERS OFTEN EMPLOY THE wave metaphor to delineate distinctions within the twentieth-century Pentecostal/Charismatic movement. David Barrett mentions three waves: Pentecostal renewal, Charismatic renewal, and a "third wave of non-Pentecostal, non-charismatic, but neo-charismatic renewal."[1] Mark Hutchinson finds the term, waves, problematic and lacking in explanatory power, and yet, he describes the waves of Pentecostalism as follows: the first wave or classic Pentecostalism links to Azusa Street, the second wave charismatic renewal emerged as classic Pentecostalism interacted with mainline denominations, followed by the self-identified "Third Wave" churches associated with the Vineyard and others that emerged from youth revivals. "Most people acknowledge the fact that the categories are hazy at the edges."[2]

Pentecostal Theologian Amos Yong (instead of waves) uses types, then names the same three categories that most scholars use: classic, charismatic-renewal, and neo-charismatic for the third wave as a miscellaneous category incorporating fourth wave impulses. It is worth examining the influence of the previous, yet

1. Barrett, *Century of the Holy Spirit*, 379.
2. Hutchinson, "The Problem with 'Waves,'" 34–54.

present and successive, four waves.[3] Todd Johnson similarly uses three categories: Pentecostals (Type 1), Charismatics (Type 2), and Independent Charismatics (Type 3). Again, the third category functions as a catch-all for fourth wave observations. All three types compose a supergroup termed, *Renewalists*, which number well over half a billion people worldwide.[4]

Pentecostalism has entered a fourth wave.[5] Church historian Ryan Reeves believes the needed historical perspective is lacking to assess this adequately but notes a potential existence of a current rise of a Fourth Wave marked by an "increased desire for intellectual credibility, thoughtfulness . . . a real substantive change that we are seeing in more Pentecostal and Charismatic influenced universities and academic settings."[6] Nonetheless, a fourth wave began in the late twentieth century[7] along with evidence of a discernable fourth wave cresting, breaking, and beaching. Well into the twenty-first century, with retrospection, there is enough historical perspective for clarification of each of the previous three waves to provide insight to ride this fourth wave of the Spirit, strategically.

Since waves are in academic literature's common parlance, this work uses the waves metaphor with the clarification in this section. This book stipulates that the timeframes of the waves are fuzzy, overlaps exist, crisp categorizations are problematic, and the waves recede but do not wash away entirely. Nevertheless, with an open reading of the scholarship, one can see four periods, each of which began in the twentieth century and continues. When one overlays the contributions of women within twentieth-century Pentecostalism—combined with church history, communication techniques, media distribution, and sociological influences—a distinctive, more accurate defining of the waves appears, which serves future research.

---

3. Yong, *The Spirit Poured Out*, 18.

4. Miller et al., *Spirit and Power*, 319.

5. Hawkes, "Third and Fourth Wave Pentecostalism," 9.

6. Reeves, "Pentecostalism," 15:54—16:54.

7. Synan et al., *Century of the Holy Spirit*, 381.

Variation in opinion on the waves is due to how academics define the term, "Pentecostal." With its first-century biblical precedence, *Pentecostal*, thought of as a purely twentieth-century phenomenon, is a misnomer. Calvary Chapel Costa Mesa avoided the Pentecostal label and remained consonant with the first church seen in Acts 2 (see Fig. 1).

3.0.1 WAVES OF PENTECOSTALISM

20th-Century Pentecostalism ". . . on my handmaidens I will pour out . . ."				
Waves	First Wave Classic	Second Wave Charismatic Renewal	Third Wave Neo-Charismatic	Fourth Wave Network/N.A.R.
Initial Timing	1901	1945	1975	1995
Significant Women	Agnes Ozman tongues experience Sister Aimee McPherson founded Foursquare denomination and Bible College (1923) Kathryn Kuhlman's ascent (1924)	Sister Aimee's passing (1944) Kuhlman restoration (1946–7) Kuhlman as yielded vessel healer, radio and TV personality	Tammy Faye Baker and Jan Crouch ascend as TV personalities Kuhlman's passing (1976)	Darlene Zschech becomes Worship Leader of Hillsong Joyce Meyer's *Battlefield of the Mind* is released
Media Communication	Radio	Broadcast TV	Satellite/Cable	Internet
Outpourings	Azusa Street Revival spawns Pentecostalism Fundamentalist denominationalism as restoration movement against Liberalism	Holy Spirit moves through established mainline denominations movements	Independent Megachurches proliferate Global Pentecostalism ascends	Toronto Blessing causes Vineyard split Rise of Bethel Church, Redding et al.

Fig. 1 © David L. Ream, 2023

Women figure prominently in Calvary Chapel worship. Women support music ministry and serve as worship leaders within this congregation before the Smiths arrived in late 1965.

Since CCCM's inception, women remain a part of the church's functioning. Since 1986, the first two worship leaders at CCCM continued a widespread practice in independent churches where the pastor and his wife co-led congregational worship. Women's contributions in worship range from song-leading, accompanying, songwriting, recording, performing, and service planning.

3.1 FIRST WAVE BREAKS

Women were disciples of Jesus and were present among the 120 waiting in Jerusalem for the Holy Spirit's power as Jesus promised at Acts 1:8 (cf. Acts 1:14). The Holy Spirit fell on "each one of them" (Acts 2:3) and "all" (Acts 2:4), implying both men and women. It should not surprise readers that God would pour his Spirit on women and men, given that "God is no respecter of persons" (Acts 10:34) and that He communed with Adam and Eve before the Fall in Genesis 3:1–24.

Old Testament enduements (gifting) of the Spirit given to women are seen in Miriam (Exod 15:20) and Deborah (Judg 4:4) and others. God's position (stated through Moses) in Numbers 11:29 sets the biblical pattern that carries through the Bible: "Enviest thou for my sake? would God that all the Lord's people were prophets, *and* that the Lord would put his spirit upon them!" Old Testament enduements of power were often given situationally as with Bezaleel and Aholiab, to construct the Tabernacle (Exod 35:30–35). Men were the norm for the endowment of the Holy Spirit, but not exclusive.

Peter's sermon on the birthday of the Church explains that the experience affecting men and women was the fulfillment of Joel's prophecy (Joel 2:28–29). Peter explains the fulfillment:

> And it shall come to pass in the last days, saith God, I will pour out of my Spirit upon all flesh: and your sons and your daughters shall prophesy, and your young men shall see visions, and your old men shall dream dreams: And on my servants and on my handmaidens I will pour

out in those days of my Spirit; and they shall prophesy
(Acts 2:17–18).

His concluding remark, "to all that are far off," expresses the continuationist position:

> Then Peter said unto them, Repent, and be baptized
> every one of you in the name of Jesus Christ for the remission of sins, and ye shall receive the gift of the Holy
> Ghost. For the promise is unto you, and to your children,
> and to all that are afar off, *even* as many as the Lord our
> God shall call (Acts 2:38–39).

These scriptural references to the Spirit poured out upon
women in Acts 2 are taken as vindication of spiritual impartation to Pentecostal women such as Aimee "Sister Aimee" Semple
McPherson, Kathryn Kuhlman, Kay Smith, Darlene Zschech, and
many others (See Fig.1). A case can be made for January 1, 1901,
from Miss Agnes N. Ozman's testimony of the reception of the gift
of speaking in tongues as *xenolalia*[8] for the purpose of evangelism,
initiates the first wave of twentieth-century Pentecostalism—not
Azusa Street in 1906:

> It came into my heart to ask Brother Parham to lay his
> hands upon me that I might receive the gift of the Holy
> Spirit. It was as his hands were laid upon my head that
> the Holy Spirit fell upon me, and I began to speak in
> tongues, glorifying God. I talked several languages, and
> it was clearly manifest when a new dialect was spoken. I
> had the added joy and glory my heart longed for and a
> depth of the presence of the Lord within that I had never
> known before. It was as if rivers of living waters were
> preceeding [sic] from my innermost being.[9]

Ozman's reference to Brother Parham is Charles Fox Parham.
Parham laid hands on and prayed with Ozman to receive the gift
of tongues in that prayer meeting of his students in 1901. He also
trained William J. Seymour of the Azusa Street Revival (1906).

8. Espinosa, *William J. Seymour*, 3.
9. Garrett, "Personal Testimony."

Parham remained adamant that the gift of *xenolalia* is evidence of the Holy Spirit and an indication of worldwide evangelism, which he maintained was the gift's purpose: Parham believed the language indicated to the recipient of the gift—the people group to which the recipient should go—to serve as an evangel and proclaim the Gospel since they had received the Holy Spirit's empowerment.[10]

Another of Parham's students was Irish immigrant Robert Semple. After his training, Parham sent him on "a mission in Toronto, where he gained a reputation as a thrilling and effective preacher."[11] One Aimee Elizabeth Kennedy was converted in 1907 in Ingersoll, Canada by his revivalist preaching. "She found both Semple and his message irresistible, and in August 1908 the couple married."[12] Both husband and wife became polished revivalist preachers.

Eighteen months after the Semples were wed, Charles Parham directed them to China where Robert contracted malaria and died. Aimee—pregnant and penniless—buried her husband in China.[13] She delivered her baby there and Aimee's mother sent the fare for the widow and child to return to the United States. Eventually "Sister Aimee" Semple McPherson founded Angelus Temple in 1923—an early megachurch serving 15,000 every day. She also founded one of earliest Christian radio stations—KFSG,[14] the aforementioned LIFE Bible College and her followers further institutionalized the Foursquare denomination.[15]

At LIFE Bible College, Chuck Smith played quarterback,[16] earned a bachelor's degree in theology,[17] met his wife Kay, and graduated in 1948.[18] The Smiths married on June 19, 1948, and

10. Synan and Nelson, *Century of the Holy Spirit*, 51.

11. Scott, *Women Who Dared*, 87.

12. Sutton, *Aimee Semple McPherson*, 10.

13. Scott, *Women Who Dared*, 87.

14. Hilliker, "Pioneer L. A. Christian Station."

15. Gastón, *William J. Seymour*, 3.

16. Fourquare, "Dick Mills Shares."

17. MacIntosh and Reis, "A Venture of Faith," 9:03–9:10.

18. Meza, "Phone Interview."

ministered in eight Foursquare churches ensconced in the first-wave context in Arizona and Southern California for the next seventeen years.[19] They entered full-time ministry as first-wave practitioners, young and full of hope. As they engaged their culture and generation for Christ, God would refine them during the *Second Wave of Pentecostalism*.[20]

3.0.3 SECOND WAVE SWELLS

While all waves of twentieth-century Pentecostalism persist,[21] the earliest sightings of the second wave become noticeable during and after WWII. This mid-1940s timing emerges, when the ministries of two pioneering women from the First Wave are considered. WWII was arguably the watershed event of the twentieth century and that period contains the death of Sister Aimee Semple McPherson (1944) and the reformation of Kathryn Kuhlman (1946). When considered in conjunction with these two women, the *First Wave of Pentecostalism* had broken on the beach and hunger for spiritual renewal began.

Radio, regional TV, and itinerant evangelistic services began to support the move of the Holy Spirit. Kuhlman normalized the Spirit-filled life. "Between 1946 and 1953, Kuhlman leveraged the growing popularity of healing ministries, minimized controversy by refashioning charismatic practices to make them more palatable to the broader culture, and reestablished herself as the leader of a well-known and respected ministry."[22] The second wave of spiritual renewal emerged around and just after WWII as classic Pentecostalism interacted with Christians looking for renewed hope in their mainstream denominations carrying into the 1950s and 1960s.

---

19. Fischer, *I Remember*, 59.
20. Bartos, "Three Waves of Spiritual Renewal," 20–42.
21. Barrett, *Century of the Holy Spirit*, 382.
22. Artman, *The Miracle Lady*, 46.

The 1940s coincide with the Smiths' entrance into ministry as representatives from classic Pentecostalism. They, too, began normalizing charismatic gifting, but within a first wave denomination—being prepared by the Holy Spirit for the future "Jesus Movement" explosion. In a parallel fashion to Kuhlman, they begin their faith journey transitioning from first to second wave but distinct from Kuhlman, the Smith's remained committed to the primacy of the local church within a first wave denomination. Kuhlman and the Smiths, like Sister Aimee, recognized and leveraged the power of radio broadcasting to evangelize.

In the Post-WWII era, TV emerged as the new technological enhancement. Kuhlman was one of the first, if not the very first, to successfully harness the new medium with local TV syndication and remain cost-effective.[23] Historical perspective shows the Smiths were typical second-wave Pentecostals because of the timing and the character of their ministry. They entered the ministry in post-WWII America, adapting to changes within their culture as they followed the Holy Spirit's leading within the Foursquare denomination in the mid-twentieth century. The character of their ministry normalized a Spirit-filled life exemplified by grounding experience to Scripture—Scripture thereby regulating Pentecostal experience.

This parallelism to the second wave is overlooked because most scholars and researchers identify the charismatic renewal as Pentecostal elements working into and through mainline Evangelicalism and Catholicism.[24] By studying what happened outside of Pentecostalism, many researchers have not considered what the Holy Spirit did within the Pentecostal denominations and Independents. The Smiths were engaging in normalizing refinements of the second wave while serving in a first-wave context. Thus, the setting was the first wave, and yet the observable actions and attitudes paralleled second-wave nuances.

Other evidence of ministering in both waves exists. In 1947, Smith and his younger brother Paul Smith did a short evangelistic

23. Artman, *The Miracle Lady*, 67–69.

24. Synan and Nelson, *Century of the Holy Spirit*, chapters 7–9.

preaching tour while both were in Bible college—an impulse consonant with the youth movement beginning during WWII[25]—linking first-wave revivalism with the second wave of charismatic renewal at the dawning of the youth movement. Beginning in June of 1948 in Prescott, Arizona, Chuck and Kay Smith took pastorates in a series of churches within their denomination.[26] Smith learned to build Jesus' church in Jesus' way in two-to-three-year stints often full of trial-and-error failures and successes. They authentically exemplified Spirit-led living in all facets of life, and post-WWII America was ready to embrace spiritual renewal. Yet, they went unseen because their example was lived out in the local church.

Due to the enormous interest generated by radio and TV ministries and personalities—e.g., Oral Roberts, Rex Humbard, and Jack Coe, the Smiths' ministry in local first-wave churches is overlooked. However, Smith's approach mirrors Kuhlman's—each independent of the other. Kuhlman in the Pittsburg/Youngstown area on a local television station was "gently exposing the television audience to divine healing through the method of personal testimony; Kuhlman offered a comfortably mediated experience of charismatic Christianity."[27] Television was new, and her approach significantly affected charismatic Christianity, starting regionally with "Your Faith and Mine" and then nationwide with "I Believe in Miracles."[28] Television shows caught the eye and garnered national attention.

Smith, not a faith healer, nonetheless like Kuhlman taught that the gifts of the Holy Spirit are available, because the Holy Spirit who inspired the Scriptures is still ministering as social historian John S. Knox explains:

> Based on the living testimonies of over a billion of believers worldwide, can one say that all the gifts of the Holy Spirit have stopped? People are still convicted and comforted. Discernment still occurs. Healings still happen.

25. "Reaching People Everywhere Since 1944."
26. Guzik, "Remembering Chuck Smith," 11:00.
27. Artman, *The Miracle Lady*, 70.
28. Artman, *The Miracle Lady*, 70.

> People still prophesy. The Holy Spirit still calls out for
> people in the world to draw close to God in Jesus Christ
> to find true love and forgiveness. The Holy Spirit has
> never ceased in His efforts to implement the plan of God,
> and as a faithful member of the Godhead, the Holy Spirit
> will never abandon God's followers. Just don't forget—Je-
> sus lovingly promised us this.[29]

The Smith's began to uncover an authentic Spirit-filled life—a biblical expression charismatic, but unlike the Charismatic Renewal
characteristic of second-wave Pentecostalism. Kuhlman, through
syndication, pushed into the limelight and homes of mainline denomination adherents dissimilar to the Smiths who served in the
shade of a Pentecostal denominational church.

With over seventy years of perspective, it appears evident that
God similarly positioned Smith and Kuhlman to obtain hope for
daily living by the overflow of the Spirit and the example set by
Jesus and the Scriptures. The Smith's normalized a Spirit-led life
grounded in the word of God and the Love of God. Some observers have charged Smith's gentler, kinder yet biblical example of life
in the Spirit as quenching the Holy Spirit. He was open to appealing to the broadest possible audience allowing the supernatural
beauty of Jesus' love to flow forth in a real-world faith walk of
testing and trusting. As he grew in ministry, relying on Jesus, the
church grew. When he relied on himself, stagnation occurred. The
Smiths surfed on both sets of waves.

3.3 THIRD WAVE RISES

It is commonly (yet incorrectly) asserted that Calvary Chapel
is of the third wave, partly due to the sociological observations
that recognize the explosion of the "Jesus Movement" in the late
1960s–1970s, as a youth movement. Researcher Mark Hutchinson
states that the *Third Wave* began as a self-identified denomination
of churches primarily associated with the Vineyard movement.[30]

29. Knox, "Spiritual Side."
30. Hutchinson, "Problem with 'Waves,'" 34–54.

Synan adds, "It originated at Fuller Theological Seminary in 1981 under the classroom ministry of John Wimber, founder of the Association of Vineyard Churches. This "wave" was comprised of mainline evangelicals who experienced signs and wonders but who disdained labels such as 'Pentecostal' or 'charismatic.' The Vineyard was the most visible movement of this category."[31]

The Vineyard movement, linked with John Wimber's leadership, originated the third wave. Calvary Chapel is occasionally or mistakenly labeled, "third wave," because Kenn Gulliksen, a Calvary Chapel ordained pastor, planted the first church to carry the name, "The Vineyard."[32] Miller correctly notes, "Gulliksen planted the original Vineyard in 1974. Ordained by Calvary Chapel in 1971 . . . Gulliksen's Vineyard, the church plant, is not equivalent to Wimber's Vineyard, the denomination."[33] Since the *Third Wave* label often functions for researchers as a catch-all term, this led researchers to equivocate CCCM as *Third Wave*. Miller (inaccurately) states, "Calvary Chapel was founded in 1965 by Chuck Smith as a ministry for hippies and surfers."[34] For clarity, it is essential to reiterate that Pastor Floyd Nelson (not Chuck Smith) founded Calvary Chapel in 1961 (not 1965) in a senior-citizens trailer park to hold Bible studies for the elderly—hardly a ministry for hippies and surfers.

Thomas Higgins notes that seven of ten distinguishing, characteristic points of Gulliksen's church plant called, "The Vineyard," were already in place as Gulliksen the founder handed the church to Wimber's leadership who can be called the "Father of the Vineyard movement."[35] Wimber credits C. Peter Wagner as having "coined the term, 'third wave,' to describe this group."[36] In order to catch this third wave of the Spirit, Wimber instructs: "The Third Wave emphasizes the universal priesthood of all Christians. The

31. Synan and Nelson, *Century of the Holy Spirit*, 18.

32. Higgins, "Founding of the Vineyard Movement," 208–28.

33. Miller, *Reinventing American Protestantism*, 46.

34. Miller, *Reinventing American Protestantism*, 19.

35. Higgins, "Founding of the Vineyard Movement," 208–28.

36. Wimber and Springer, *Power Evangelism*, 171.

only requirements to ride that wave are a hunger for God and a humility to receive Him on His terms."[37]

Although the original Vineyard church affiliated with CCCM as a movement, it distinguished itself apart from Calvary Chapel. The self-referential impulses of the *Third Wave* is consonant with Post-Modernism[38] and antithetical to the independent nature of Calvary Chapel. Wimber's desire and decision to proclaim his new work as a denomination marks the point of departure between the paradigmatic Calvary Chapel model of the Jesus movement and the postmodern Vineyard Movement.

Wimber and Smith (as leaders) each attending to their unique calling, subsequently distanced the Vineyard as *Third Wave* from Calvary Chapel of the *Second Wave* without animosity. Since Smith and Wimber are Fundamentalists, this parting of the ways is more amicable than the sharpness and splintering that characterized the Fundamentalist versus Modernist debate of the 1920s and 1930s.

Unfortunately, the emphasis on experiencing the Holy Spirit at the Vineyard came at the expense of relaxing the centrality of teaching and the authority of the word of God. This subtle shift of epistemological sources and priority led to a parting of the ways—the Vineyard went from a CCCM affiliated church to become a self-proclaimed denomination. As Fromm states:

> About 40 Calvary Chapel outreach pastors joined Wimber in the foundation of the Vineyard denomination, which was ultimately promoted as a "Third Wave" of the Holy Spirit . . . Kenn Gulliksen, Tom Stipe, Mark Foreman, and several other pastors who had ventured to follow Wimber into the "power paradigm" eventually returned back to a text-centered model based upon the wisdom doxology as practiced by Calvary Chapel. As Foreman says simply, "Signs and wonders follow."[39]

Foreman's "signs and wonders" comment turns out to be a significant reference that acknowledges Wimber's pursuit of the

37. Wimber and Springer, *Power Evangelism*, 175.
38. Smith Jr., *End of the World*, 31.
39. Fromm, "Textual Communities," 282–83.

signs and wonders as equal to or more important than the authority of Scripture. This runs counter to the biblical pattern of ministry that Smith held as shown in Acts 8 where the "preaching of the word" (Acts 8:4–5) precedes miracles (Acts 8:6–7), leading to joy (Acts 8:8), which exemplifies the biblical pattern of CCCM's pattern of ministry.

This seemingly minor detail was a major point of departure and indicates the meticulous attention to the details of the text and its inherent authority that regulated the working of the Spirit through the church according to Pastor Smith's practice. Having gone independent years earlier, Smith intentionally positioned CCCM's affiliated churches apart from Wimber's vision of a Vineyard denomination. Wimber's quest for a new denomination[40] ran counter to Smith's decision to maintain independence from a central denomination.[41] On the surface, what seemed adiaphora (things indifferent) became an amicable break. Rather than splinter, Smith and Wimber sought the more excellent way of love to prevail (1 Cor 12:31—13:13) and understood Christ was the final judge.

In addition to the word of God as the pre-eminent epistemological foundation that has precedence before the signs and wonders of God, another doctrinal difference results from differing views of eschatology. Wimber and many Third-Wave congregations often teach a derivative of George Ladd's *Kingdom Now!*, claiming, "The blessings of the Lord's kingdom were available to the faithful at any time, through prayer worship in the Spirit."[42] Smith, however, was a staunch premillennial dispensationalist, emphasizing an imminent expectation of the church's rapture to meet Christ in the air. These eschatological interpretations influence the direction of the human role to advance diverging paths to achieve God's aim—"Your will be done on earth as it is in heaven" (Matt 6:10).

The centrality of the inerrant word of God led to Smith issuing a non-condemning position letter to Calvary Chapel affiliated

---

40. Hawkes, "Third and Fourth Wave Pentecostalism," 117.

41. Miller, *Reinventing American Protestantism*, 36.

42. Fromm, "Textual Communities," 284.

pastors considering to "go Vineyard" with their churches. In part, Smith offered, "If you desire to emphasize the experience aspects of the work of the Holy Spirit, it would probably be well if you would seek an affiliation with Pentecostal Churches, Assemblies of God, Foursquare, or Church of God because they seem to have a more experience-oriented type of ministry."[43]

The Vineyard denomination marks the origin of the third wave. Thus, the Calvary Chapel movement preceding the Vineyard movement is not third-wave. Calvary Chapel as a movement, stands with the Vineyard denomination in their devotion to Christ, but doxologically distinct in practice. Some scholars miss this fine distinction that divides the spiritual impulses of the *Second and Third Waves*. Calvary Chapel and the Vineyard shared Gulliksen's original desire for intimacy with Christ in a dynamic, loving, personal relationship made possible by Jesus' redemptive work. Nevertheless, they amicably separated with Wimber on "differences of doctrine, style, worship, and most importantly authority that developed over time."[44]

Wimber and Wagner taught that its leaders, anointed with power and authority, are on par with the apostles and the prophets in Scripture. This theme of personal authority equivalent to Scripture is one that some leaders within the *Fourth Wave* uncritically implement into their present-day expressions of ministry and is a domain worthy of critical review and revision when examining the *Fourth Wave*.

3.4 FOURTH WAVE IN THE SPIN CYCLE?

The *Fourth Wave* appears to be composed of at least two divergent strains, sometimes at odds with the other. One strain engages the academic community, securing and explicating its Pentecostal foundations. The second impulse pursues passionate worship and the manifestation of gifts of the Spirit for personal fulfillment and

43. Paul Smith, *New Evangelicalism*, 136.

44. Fromm, "Textual Communities," 284.

evangelism. An early 1991 announcement of a *Fourth Wave* awareness conference focuses on

> Pentecostal/charismatic movements in different regions of the world . . . The ability of the movements to cross ethnic, racial, and class barriers . . . unique thought patterns and relationship to the postmodern world . . . impact on global moral reform and culture, from a non-western perspective; The dangers of excess and heresy.[45]

The second strain of the *Fourth Wave* moves even further in spiritual excesses than does Wimber's Vineyard and beyond the working of Holy Spirit according to Scripture.

It is ironic how, Wimber—relying on biblical authority—disassociates the Vineyard denomination from the Toronto Vineyard church and the Catch the Fire movement on similar grounds as to why Smith distanced the Calvary Chapel movement from the Vineyard denomination. The Toronto Blessing became a marker of the *Fourth Wave* even more pronounced than the experiential emotionalism of the Vineyard movement.

After an inquiry into the Pentecostal body, primarily from a study of the mid-1990s Toronto Blessing and Catch the Fire movement, Michael Wilkinson opined on the human body as an experiential site for human-divine interactions when he extra-biblically asserted: "Pentecostal worship is characterized by physicality and through the kinesthetic participation of bodies in motion. Rituals associated with spirits that are dualistic between the Holy Spirit and evil spirits also characterize Pentecostalism."[46]

The dualism between the Holy Spirit and evil spirits at work in the church that Wilkinson describes is not found in Acts Chapter 2. Indeed, Smith and Wimber (raised as a Quaker) would not endorse unclean spirits at work in their churches—it would be *anathema*. As watchmen of their respective flocks, they would safeguard the spiritual activity to be exclusively consonant with

---

45. Legge, "Fourth Wave Under Study," A14.
46. Wilkinson and Althouse, "Pentecostalism," 33.

the Holy Spirit. Thus, as Smith separated from Wimber and the *Third Wave*, Wimber separated from the *Fourth Wave*.

Another point of distinction of the *Fourth Wave*, consonant with post-modernistic values, is a position of self-referential individual authority to achieve biblical ends by people who set personal authority above or on par with the Biblical text. For many of these newly self-appointed apostles hold the view: "Without the authority of today's apostles, the church cannot fulfill its mission of transforming societies and advancing God's kingdom."[47]

Fourth Wave strains share historical precedents with the former three waves at the surface level, which sociologists and anthropologists observe, minus spiritual insight. The born-again researcher aims wholistically—realizing that not all spiritual activity is Christian and God-honoring merely because it is spiritual. The purely atomistic training of many anthropological and sociological researchers lacks the apparatus to discern among spirits (1 Cor 12:10), and thus they equivocate the testimony and experiences of spiritually engaged or emotionally charged participants with worshipping in Spirit and in truth (John 4:24).

In the domain of Christian worship, not all spirits are equal. The Bible acknowledges unclean spirits are at work in this world as well as one, and only one, Holy Spirit. 1 Samuel 16:14–16, 23; Zechariah 13:2; Matthew 12:43; Mark 1:23, 26; 3:30; 5:2, 8; 7:25; Luke 4:33; 8:29; 9:42; 11:24 and other passages acknowledge a spiritual world at work within the material world.

Scriptural understanding and a biblical worldview lens are necessary to observe Christian spiritual experience and to discriminate among spirits in the manner that retains the spiritual sensitivity that Chuck Smith as the lead pastor exemplified. The Bible admits that there are deceiving spirits and psychology admits that there exist extreme human emotional impulses that may appear as having a spiritual nature without regard to holiness. The two strains within the *Fourth Wave* are unfolding in time before postmodern eyes. The historical relationship of the lead pastor and

47. Geivett and Pivec, *New Apostolic Reformation?*, 74.

worship leader at CCCM provides a foundational, biblical understanding of spiritual authority within God's Kingdom.

3.5 SMITH'S TRANSFORMATION

Inerrancy and literal interpretation account for the biblical position Pastor Smith held. At CCCM, one constant—the inerrancy of
scripture, literally interpreted—was the basis for Smith's position on
theological issues central or peripheral—e.g., the worship of God,
evangelism, prayer, speaking in tongues, a dispensational eschatology, and the manifestation of God's love by living in the Spirit.

Smith taught and lived the doctrine of imminency. Since Jesus
commanded, "Be ready" (Matt 24:44; Luke 12:40), Smith biblically
advanced an authentic obedience to the faith in the Scriptures as
a witness to his culture. To keep unity, he would leave room for
the Gospel of Jesus to work subjectively in the lives of believers
and not disparage fruitful ministry. Thus, one branch of fruitful
ministry was not exalted over another.

Within his former denomination, at a weekly prayer meeting, Smith received a "word of knowledge" (1 Cor 12:8), Smith
claims, "The Lord said he was changing my name to 'Shepherd'
because He was going to make me the shepherd of many flocks
and the church would not be large enough to hold all the people
who would be flocking to hear the Word of God."[48] This prophetic
word is one of God's spoken word gifts to guide Pastor Smith in the
ministry. He released personal preferences to uphold Scripture. He
positioned CCCM to minister God's love and grace. He preferred
to link CCCM historically to the first century church of Acts above
the Reformation.

With his mother's passing, the Holy Spirit led Smith to become independent of the Foursquare denomination.[49] Eventually,
he planted an independent church: The Corona Christian Center,
in Corona, California. Initially, Smith saw it as the beginning of

48. Smith and Brooke, *Harvest*, 23.

49. Peretski and Peretski, *What God Hath Wrought*, 51:47—52:10.

the fulfillment of the second part of that prophetic word he had received, because the church was growing and was a ministry that supported a Pastor and his family. However, the first part of the prophecy was yet unfulfilled since this was only one church and not many flocks. By 1964–65, this church materially provided for Smith and his family. Smith no longer needed to be a bi-vocational pastor. Could he have asked himself the question he posed at his Bible Study years later, as Miller noted, "God, what are you trying to tell me?"[50]

During the pastorate in Corona, Smith was also teaching a mid-week Bible class in Costa Mesa. The Costa Mesa group encouraged Smith to relocate there. In Corona, about this same time, he encountered human resistance to a simple change of form in worship. An elder, who also served occasionally as a song leader, insisted on keeping the chairs in rows while Pastor Smith wanted to arrange the chairs in a "circle for a Sunday night study . . . a more relational setting for the kind of gathering and the number of people attending."[51]

The Corona congregation warmly responded to Smith's response to the Lord's leading. Smith sensed that changing the chairs that night was of the Lord for the good of His people. However, Smith's board did not approve of the move and restricted Smith's freedom to minister as the Spirit led him to minister. Smith reflects: "I'm not going to be under these kinds of restrictions I must be open to be led by the Spirit. So, when we came to Calvary Chapel and established, the bylaws, we didn't create a Presbyterian form of government. It was more of an *Episkopos* form of government for Calvary Chapel."[52]

Smith's willingness to respond to the Holy Spirit on Sunday nights in Corona before coming to CCCM, indicates he was not entrenched in tradition. It is additional evidence that he aligns with the second wave of charismatic renewal, allowing the Holy Spirit freedom to minister individually among people. The board's

---

50. Miller, *Reinventing American Protestantism*, 31.

51. Fromm, "Textual Communities," 152.

52. Smith, *Calvary Chapel Distinctives*, 26.

resistance to Smith's leadership style in Corona was not present among those in Costa Mesa.

Around this same time, the pre-existing independent church, Calvary Chapel Costa Mesa had received a prophecy that a pastor would visit and eventually accept the call to pastor this church. He will want to make changes to the building, especially the pulpit area. Finally, God would bless this pastor's ministry, and this church would have a worldwide impact.[53] Smith seemed to confirm the prophetic word given to the CCCM congregation when he began making suggestions to renovate the building that paralleled the details of the prophecy. They received his ideas, as confirming a word of prophecy that they had received before Smith's arrival as a guest preacher/teacher.

After that first Sunday morning, the congregation was excited to see what God might be doing with their little church. The congregation left the prophecy unknown to Smith at that time; yet, the Holy Spirit was using circumstances on both sides of the pastor/congregation equation, stirring Smith's heart to take the struggling, independent church since founding pastor Floyd Nelson was retiring.

Smith came to CCCM as an Assistant Pastor in November 1965 seeking to lead a church as the Holy Spirit was leading him, "and to offer Christ's love instead of respectability and conformity."[54] Smith preferred to forego the stability and security he had achieved in Corona to pursue authentically the Lord's leading. He guided the worship service with the Bible, prayer, and hymnal. Kay, his wife, often accompanied Smith on piano. In June of 1966, CCCM also purchased an organ to supplement the piano accompaniment.[55]

Smith called the numbers from the hymnal each Sunday morning to support the theme of the teaching and led congregational singing. "He immediately established the principle that no verse would be left out when the congregation would sing a hymn

53. Guzik, "Remembering Chuck Smith."

54. Smith and Brooke, *Harvest*, 33.

55. Fromm, "Textual Communities," 150.

. . . as well as take the time to explain the meaning when introducing hymns unfamiliar to the congregation."[56] He would only sing a solo before teaching if someone else led congregational singing. Thus, Smith's teaching style and liturgy pattern originated from his *First Wave* tradition but moderated to be accessible in a non-denominational setting where Evangelicals, Fundamentalists, and Pentecostals of all varieties could find the freedom to pursue a life in the Spirit clearly defined by Scripture.

Smith purposely selected songs out of the hymnal to produce a synergistic effect with the Sunday morning teaching. His teaching style was careful to distinguish between expositing on Sunday nights and expounding, which he called his teaching work on Sunday morning. "These two methods, exposition and expounding, should go hand in hand: they are two sides of the same coin."[57] Like the music, the teaching differed on Sunday mornings. A visitor or a family new to town would find the CCCM Sunday morning service familiar and similar to mid-twentieth-century mainline evangelical denominational expressions of worship.

December 5, 1965, Smith began his tenure at CCCM[58] as "associate pastor to be responsible for all teaching ministry."[59] Pastor Nelson provided oversight during the transition phase participating in monthly board meetings, song leading, opening meetings in prayer through "at least the first four months of 1966."[60] In the monthly board meetings, Smith immediately began "putting very practical issues into place and taking care of undone business, such as paying the gardener."[61] Smith led the church to look beyond itself supporting Wycliffe Bible Translators and Missionary Aviation Fellowship. In September of 1966, Smith was unanimously selected

56. Fromm, "Textual Communities," 154.

57. Smith and Nixon, *Line Upon Line*, 19.

58. Fischer, *I Remember*, 56.

59. Fromm, "Textual Communities," 147.

60. Fromm, "Textual Communities," 148.

61. Fromm, "Textual Communities," 150.

as Senior Pastor. He summarized the first two years at CCCM as "years of peace and quiet in which we saw moderate growth."[62]

Original board member Sharon Gardner Fischer recalls: "An interesting observation is the fact that Calvary Chapel had more than quadrupled in size before the Jesus People Movement came into existence, which further substantiates that the Church's growth stemmed from the preaching of God's Word."[63] Smith went from evangelistic preaching to expository teaching while ministering in denominational churches in Huntington Beach and Los Serranos as well as further refinements in independent churches and home Bible studies. He writes, "I discovered the spiritual growth that occurred in people was a result of simply reading through the Bible and teaching what God had inspired."[64]

In the Jesus movement of the late 1960s and 1970s, CCCM's unique approach, melding the objective Holy Scripture with the subjective work of the Holy Spirit, attracted the hippies and those dissatisfied with *status quo* Christianity who were seeking a tangible relationship with Jesus Christ. God spiritually prepared CCCM through the working of the Holy Spirit and the counsel of the Holy Bible to meet the needs of those hungering and thirsting after God in that generation.

62. Smith, *Memoir*, 162.

63. Fischer, *I Remember*, 69.

64. Smith, *Memoir*, 117.

4

Here Come the Hippies

PASTOR SMITH'S DISCOVERY RELATED to the spiritual growth that comes from feeding on the word of God and the subsequent re-forging of his style of ministry consonant with spiritual renewal combine with changes in American culture, world events, global communication, and Kay Smith's heart for young people. These impulses in the hearts of the couple attending to the will of God responding to their surrounding culture transform them into *Papa Chuck* and *Mama Kay*. They begin to reach out and minister to the spiritually starving young people—the same age as their children, whom the media has dubbed hippies. Calvary Chapel Costa Mesa grew before the hippies. First, the hippies trickled in and soon a deluge of human souls arrived, finding the true love and peace that originally drove them on their spiritual journey.

The "Summer of Love"[1] in 1967 did not produce hippies; it merely revealed a generation already searching for peace and love. They left their parents' homes, realizing the hollowness of optimism in modernity. They had experienced materialism, ap-preciated the creature comforts of having basic human needs met and enjoyed the freedom to explore human consciousness, and yet, they yearned for and sought a spiritually fulfilling life. The

1. Howard, "Flowering Hippie Movement," 382.

"Angel-headed hipsters burning for the ancient heavenly connection to the starry dynamo in the machinery of night"[2] quickly learned through cold experience that the machinations of darkness and the promises of the drug culture were false hope that could not bring lasting fulfillment.

Greg Laurie explains, "There were two distinct Americas. One was the conventional, achievement-driven, work-ethic world that had followed the '50s, populated mostly by people over the age of thirty. The other was a growing youth counterculture that . . . embraced the planet, higher consciousness, and alternative realities . . . freedom was the ultimate high."[3]

Nevertheless, centuries before, the Holy Spirit had already imparted the resolution to King Solomon that God had "made everything appropriate in its time. He also placed eternity within them—yet, no person can fully comprehend what God is doing from beginning to end" (Eccl 3:11 ISV). God bridged the generation gap of the two Americas through the Holy Spirit illuminating the word of God to a listening audience. The Holy Spirit originally inspired the creation of the biblical text, and he also illuminates the hearers of that same word, demonstrating what God wants for each generation. Historical perspective gives the curious a glimpse of comprehension of what God was doing in 1967 that led to the Jesus movement in the late 1960s.

4.1 POP GOES THE MAMAS AND THE PAPAS

The pop group, *The Mamas and the Papas*, had the 1966 single of the year with "California Dreamin.'"[4] Co-written by "Mama" Michelle and "Papa" John Phillips, the lyrics contrast a cold winter day to the warmth of California—luring the listeners to come out west. Initially, it was San Francisco and not Los Angeles that

---

2. Ginsberg, *Howl and Other Poems*, 1956.

3. Laurie and Vaughn, *Jesus Revolution*, 27.

4. Billboard, "Top Records of 1966," 34.

became the focal point for gathering as America's young people learned of the "Human Be-In: on January 14, 1967.[5]

That day (a sunny 66° F)—the warmest day of January that year in San Francisco—idealized images of a warm, sunny Saturday in the park where harmless, beautiful people peacefully protested California's outlawing of LSD on October 6, 1966. The harsh reality was that the coldest temperature of that January was 36° F with three other days at 37° F and an average temperature of the month at 48.93° F.[6] Oblivious to facts, many young people were captivated by the inaccurate media portrayal of that day.

At least 20,000 people gathered that day in Golden Gate Park where Timothy Leary instructed the audience to "Tune in, turn on and drop out."[7] The images of peace-loving people enjoying life and each other became an existential piece of evidence that California was the place to be, even if it was only one day. Kopp explains, "The event went off largely without a hitch; apparently, there were no arrests, and despite the massive crowds, at the conclusion of the festivities, the park was relatively litter-free . . . In many ways, the relatively spontaneous Human Be-In was the spark that lit the fires of the Summer of Love."[8] Summer Solstice began on June 21, 1967, but at least two more songs and one media event led to the *Summer of Love.*

Papa John Phillips capitalized on the ideal. He also wrote the anthemic, "San Francisco (Be Sure to Wear Flowers in Your Hair)." Scott MacKenzie's version was released on May 13, 1967. The song promised that many gentle people and a love-in would be there that summer in San Francisco.[9] The song raced up the charts to its peak position in July,[10] but the social reality was a let-down. The promise to restless youth of a love-in was too alluring to resist.

5. Wolfgang, "Human Be-In."

6. "San Bruno, CA Weather History."

7. Kopp, "Free Love & LSD."

8. Kopp, "Free Love & LSD."

9. Phillips, "San Francisco."

10. "Billboard Hot 100."

Another highly influential and significant song was "All You Need is Love" by The Beatles. The BBC made this the first pop song broadcast live on TV around the world—a global phenomenon—which represented the anti-war spirit and the *grooviness* of swinging London.[11] John and Paul sang with flowers in their hair, perpetuating the optimism of the song and the era of flower power while George and Ringo performed, backed, and surrounded with flowers. John wrote the song between May 22 and its live performance on the TV program, "Our World," on June 25. The television event certainly set a mood of optimism for the *Summer of Love.*

Human optimism relies on a tendency to take a favorable view of human success despite human fallibility. This is an inferior substitute for biblical hope, which is a desirable expectation that relies on The Almighty. The Beatle sentiment—All you need is love—is a beautiful thought to think, but is it true to reality? The world was indeed shrinking due to global communication and jet plane travel. The times were changing, but was the world improving? The two-and-a-half-hour TV program, "Our World," carefully scripted and supported, showed our world becoming qualitatively different. Although it espoused peace and love, which are indeed noble values, (in retrospect) the reality was only a façade.

Returning to California, the Monterrey Pop Festival (June 16–18, 1967) shared with the world the proposition that experiencing music augmented with drug use could indeed change human existence, by changing individual people from the inside out. Yet, the festival could not change fallen human nature. Although it was wildly successful from a commercial music perspective, rock critic, historian, and Britannica contributor Ed Ward concluded, "A 1968 festival was scrapped when it was discovered that the proceeds and the festival company's bookkeeper had vanished."[12]

The editors of History.com similarly assess, "The Summer of Love that followed Monterey may have failed to usher in a lasting era of peace and love, but the festival introduced much of the

---

11. Watts, "The Beatles and All You Need."

12. Ed Ward, "The Monterey Pop Festival"

music that has come to define that particular place and time."[13] It may have been fun, but it did not, and it could not produce the fruit of the Spirit.

Mimicry of the Christian church that Jesus said he would build (Matt 16:18) created a counterfeit spiritual experience that left thousands of young people disillusioned, and many of its leading voices dead within a few years. *The Mamas and the Papas* typify the entropy of the era. In 2007, journalist Ben Sisario (with historical perspective) wrote, "In reality, they were a destructive tangle of love affairs, accompanied by plenty of drugs and alcohol."

In Sisario's article, he quotes "Papa" Denny Doherty: "It was an untenable situation, Cass wanted me, I wanted Michelle, John wanted Michelle, Michelle wanted me, she wanted her freedom."[14] Craig Morrison's entry on the *Mamas and the Papas* concludes, "One year after 1967's Monterey Pop Festival, masterminded largely by John Phillips and [Lou] Adler, the group disbanded, reforming briefly in 1971. Elliot, who became a soloist, died prematurely. The Phillipses divorced."[15]

The *ecclesia* that Jesus Christ died to create (Eph 4:3–6) is a group composed of forgiven individuals, born-again (John 3:5–8), Spirit-filled and Spirit-baptized into one body of Christ (1 Cor 12:13). They live by the Spirit and do not carry out the human desires of the flesh (Gal 5:16–26). The word of God (Heb 4:12) and the Spirit of Christ (Rom 8:9) enable the *ecclesia* to grow in purity and produce the ninefold fruit of the Spirit (Gal 5:22–23). Bearing fruit or spiritual fruitfulness and "indicates beauty, spontaneity, quietness, and growth rather than effort, labor, strain, and toil. Scripture's use of the fruit . . . suggests unity and coherence in the outworking of these virtues."[16] *The Mamas and the Papas* were a microcosm of baseless optimism, grounded in the finite power of humanity and ignoring actual consequences, which countered biblical truth and reality, leading to the ruination of humans.

13. "Monterey Pop Festival Reaches Climax."
14. Sisario, "Denny Doherty."
15. Morrison, "Mamas and the Papas."
16. Jeremiah, "Fruit of the Spirit."

4.2 MAMA KAY AND PAPA CHUCK

Nonetheless, a generation of seekers remained, yearning for the true spiritual fulfillment that only the love of God supplies. There, near the Southern California beaches, was another mama and papa cooperating with the love of God, the Holy Spirit, and the word of God. God had been preparing them over seventeen years in ministry to share the Prince of Peace with a generation seeking peace and love.

Kay and Chuck Smith were near Huntington Beach taking their family out to celebrate their oldest daughter Jeanette's high school graduation in 1967. It was Kay who first spotted young people, about the age of her own children, spaced-out on drugs. The heart of a mother, moved with compassion, began praying for them. She told Chuck, "Honey we've got to reach these kids. We are going to lose this generation. They just need Jesus."[17]

CCCM went from about 25 to 100 people by October 1967 and transitioned to two Sunday morning services as they looked for a place with greater seating capacity.[18] Smith initially eschewed the hippie lifestyle but eventually opted to reach out to them with the unity of the Spirit (Eph 4:13), biblically attending to faith, hope, and love (1 Cor 13:13). The hippies in San Francisco faithfully hanging on in false hope sensed that love remained elusive as they eked out the remains of the delightfully warm October.[19]

By December, the average temperature in San Francisco was 48.05° F.[20] Their worn-out welcome and months of homelessness left the hippies with few peaceful options. Some found communal housing in and around San Francisco. Some hitchhiked home or to other pursuits. Some, still hungry and thirsting after righteousness, went south to warmer Southern California. Mama Kay and Papa Chuck would be welcoming the spiritually hungry for a consistent feeding on the word of God.

17. Beeler, "Generation Led to Jesus," 7.
18. Fischer, *I Remember*, 73.
19. "San Bruno, CA Weather History."
20. "San Bruno, CA Weather History."

The Smiths, unlike the pop group, relied on God's resources. The Jesus movement showed that actual spiritual fulfillment could come from a worship relationship with the true and living God. This worship relationship with humanity is the great purpose of God for His creation of humanity. Real spiritual satisfaction for many of these hippies was realized in Southern California at an independent, non-denominational church named Calvary Chapel Costa Mesa where Papa Chuck and Mama Kay had been refining their ministry of a Holy-Spirit filled life according to the Scriptures.

5

Jesus Music and the Jesus Movement

In 2012, Chuck Smith, reflecting over the course of his service to the Lord, stated, "The more I studied, the more positive I became, and more convinced of the fact that Jesus Christ is indeed, God's revelation of Himself to man and that He is the Son of God and that through Him I can know God intimately, and personally. That is why I can testify of a personal, intimate relationship with God. He made that possible."[1] This statement of knowledge blends *a priori* (reason and logic) and *a posteriori* or experiential knowledge.

The knowledge Smith refers to by study and a personal intimate relationship encapsulates what the hippies found in their search to address the spiritual lack that they had discovered was absent from the purely material lifestyle. They found that God is real and can be known experientially through Jesus Christ as presented from the Holy Scriptures and the Holy Spirit at work in daily living. They also found reason to abandon the false hope in attempting to attain a God-consciousness, an altered state of awareness, or an ascetic lifestyle. Their changed lives further evidenced that God is real and can be known.

---

1. Peretski and Peretski, *What God Hath* Wrought, 3:00–3:30.

Smith's ministry both preceded and succeeded what popular media termed, "The Jesus Revolution"[2] or the Jesus movement. This movement was far more than what occurred at Calvary Chapel Costa Mesa. Nonetheless, Smith became known as the Father of the Jesus movement as result of the fruit that remains (John 15:16), which came out of ministry that relied on God and His resources to meet the spiritual needs of people. The lasting fruit is the worldwide proliferation of churches and missions that results from relying on Christ to build His church as He said He would (Matt 16:18).

5. 1 WORSHIP LEADING BEFORE AND DURING THE MOVEMENT

Pastor Chuck Smith initially led worship, singing, and teaching seventeen years before the "Jesus Movement" and the "Jesus Music" originated. Internationally known evangelist and megachurch pastor, Greg Laurie, attended CCCM Sunday morning services and agreed the hippies learned and sang hymns even though many had been unchurched.[3] Smith led the congregation in song from the hymnal with traditional piano and organ arrangements even after he hired a full-time worship leader from 1985 forward. The weeknight pattern of the now ubiquitous praise band was common in the subsequent network of Calvary Chapel affiliates for Sunday mornings. However, CCCM declined to implement contemporary Christian music on Sunday mornings.

In the 1970s, contemporary Christian music gained traction to compete with other forms of sacred music.[4] However, the Sunday morning service at CCCM went through the Jesus movement without worship wars and remained traditional. Researcher Jonathon Dueck offers an explanation behind this reality that may prove helpful in stabilizing global movements and guiding textual

---

2. Laurie, and Vaughn, *Jesus Revolution*, 136.
3. Peretski and Peretski, *What God Hath Wrought*, 1:14:33–56.
4. Perez, "Beyond the Guitar," 18–26.

communities away from constantly chasing after trends: "Church music (and all music) is inescapably a negotiated social practice, but we need to consider it from the viewpoint of the individual taking part in this social practice to understand what is really happening."[5] Chuck Smith, as lead pastor negotiated the social practice of the Sunday Morning Worship service through practical application of Scripture in the church service.

Smith post-WWII was both lead pastor and worship leader. By the time of the Jesus movement, he had learned to resolve these and many other issues by relying on the Holy Spirit and the Holy Scriptures to guide the direction of the church. Smith had learned that reliance on the whole counsel of God and each born-again believer's personal relationship with God was the essential element of fruitful ministry. From 1946 on, Pastor Smith functioned in the roles of song leader and Bible teacher. He shared worship leading with his wife, Kay, and others in denominational and independent churches by the time the hippies arrived (late 1967 and 1968).

5.2 WORSHIP LEADING AFTER THE MOVEMENT

God worked through this fruitful ministry and launched more than a thousand churches, Bible colleges, conference centers, and revolutionized contemporary worship music as pioneers in the Contemporary Christian Music genre. Yet, the Sunday morning service had only marginally incorporated its own music. Observing only what was happening during the Sunday morning service of CCCM more than twenty years after the hippies first began arriving at CCCM, Smith continued a common order of service similar to evangelistic, Protestant church services in the U.S.A. since WWII. This intentional decision positioned CCCM within the broader range of evangelicalism and intentionally distanced them from typical Pentecostal stylings consistent with the spiritual renewal movement in evangelicalism.

---

5. Dueck, *Congregational Music*, 170.

Mama Kay and Papa Chuck Smith were the guests of honor as CCCM celebrated their twenty-fifth year of ministry at CCCM on Dec 2, 1990. From their ministry, God had launched a plethora of churches affiliated with, and yet independent from, the mother church throughout the United States and around the world. Some have playfully referred to the headwaters of this outpouring of the Holy Spirit as Calvary Chapel, Costa *Mecca*. As the closing speaker that night in 1990, Pastor Smith purposefully focusing on Christ's accomplishments remarked, "We take our hats off to the past and our jackets off for the future work God has for us."[6]

5.3 LITERATURE REVIEW WORSHIP LEADING AFTER THE JESUS MOVEMENT

The literature on the lead pastor/worship leader relationship does not identify biblical elements of fruitful ministry. CCCM in the Jesus movement provides a documented context to examine how worship elements God-to-human (vertical axis), as well as human-to-human (horizontal axis) interactions.

5.3.1 Worship Leading Literature Misses the Mark of Fruitful Ministry

Fruitful ministry is a biblical concept introduced in Genesis 1:22 to all of creation. Then, specifically to mankind, Genesis records, "And God blessed them, and God said unto them, 'Be fruitful, and multiply, and replenish the earth'" (Gen 1:28). The most detailed teaching by Jesus is found in John Chapter 15. This biblical injunction to bear fruit that remains is a command of Jesus to His disciples and a hallmark of a disciple's ministry. However, many in worship ministry may be unaware of it. Veteran researcher George Barna reports that only 19 percent of born-again Christians

---

6. Fischer, *I Remember,* 148.

possess a biblical worldview—indicating as many as 4 out of 5 worship leaders do not minister with a biblical worldview.[7]

A recent article, "Too Much Bono in the Church,"[8] guides worship leaders to stop striving for a weekly mountain top experience in favor of a balanced approach to ministering to the full range of the worship *pathos*. Too often, lead pastors select worship leaders for musical ability, not for theological acumen or their personal walk with the Lord. Research that points out problem areas, providing a negative example, does not communicate data leading to fruitful ministry. To extend the metaphor, this is only pruning. By examining the CCCM worship leaders involved in fruitful ministry over twenty to fifty years, patterns of interaction emerge as these leaders remain usable instruments in the Master's hand in ministry.

5.3.2 Marriage Analogy and Current Reality

It was common to find the lead pastor and the pastor's wife as accompanist anchoring the Sunday morning service in churches across America in the mid-twentieth century. Pastor of Music Ministry at The Shepherd's Church, Aaron Kilian spiritualizes this twentieth century reality to a broader application when he concludes, "This relationship is like a marriage; it's actually a ministry marriage. In this ministry marriage, remember that he is your authority, and you are to submit to him and serve him. In most cases, he is your boss."[9]

The marriage analogy could be helpful to those who have the experience of a successful, biblical marriage. Unfortunately, many twenty-first-century worship leaders, raised in postmodern, single-parent homes may have never witnessed holy matrimony. Thus, the analogy is hollow, and the pattern of ministry is unclear. Marriage—not biblically defined or embraced—in postmodernity, or worse, uncritically interpreted from culture, leaves the marriage

7. Barna, *American Worldview Inventory*, 12, 14.

8. Niequist, "Too Much Bono?," 42–45.

9. Kilian, "The Relationship."

analogy for the relationship between lead pastor and worship leader with limited applicability for the twenty-first-century church.

5.3.3 Biblical Perspective and Purpose Exists

Becoming the true worshippers that the Father is seeking (John 4:23–24) suggests God's goal to redeem humanity is subordinate to God's ultimate purpose of having a holy people. Scott Aniol, Executive Vice President and Editor-in-chief of G3 Ministries and Professor of Pastoral Theology at Grace Bible Theological Seminary, reports:

> (1) God's chief end is his own glory; (2) worship brings God ultimate glory, and thus creation of worshipers is the *missio Dei*; (3) although redemption is an important purpose for God's mission, it is nevertheless subordinate to the ultimate end of creating worshipers since God accomplishes his mission through redemption; (4) the *missio Dei* and the mission of the church are related, but not identical. The church's mission is to make disciples through the proclamation of God's Word so that they might draw near to communion with God through Christ by faith.[10]

5.4 WORSHIP LEADER AS DEVELOPING CONCEPT

There are discrepancies in the emerging office of the Worship Leader. Note the variance in the usage of the term, *worship leader*, in the following quotes. "If you were born after 1980, you probably don't remember when the term, *worship leader*, didn't exist. But that designation really didn't emerge until the early 1970s."[11] Contrast that with another author referring to the dawning of the MTV era of the early to mid-1980s: "I don't even think 'worship

10 Aniol, *Waters of Babylon,* 95.
11. Kauflin, *Worship Matters,* 51.

leader was even a category back then."[12] He continues, "This 1980s forerunner of the worship leader 'Hand Wavey Guy.' I mean no disrespect with this title . . . You probably had him waving those hands at you when you were growing up too."[13] These writers disagree regarding when the term arrives in church lexicon, though they agree there is an objective role. The first suggests an objective role by using designation, and the second humorously, nonetheless, notes a category suggesting an objective role.

5.4.1 Trade Journals Offer Varying Points of View

Trade journals regularly affirm the lead pastor as the primary worship leader deferring to Hebrews 13:17—"The rule over you"—as the proof-text to follow. Thought exists that both are pastors responsible and complementary, and yet the lead pastor is singly accountable to God.[14] Some have asserted that the worship leader should be fiercely loyal to the lead pastor for job security, completely ignoring the spiritual aspect.

Wahl writes, "As a worship leader, the relationship with your Senior Pastor is the most important professional relationship you have. You should guard it with all your heart. You should protect it with all your strength."[15] Reciprocally, from the lead pastor to the worship leader, Fromm notes, "As a pastor . . . You might have simple or complex spheres of authority. You might stand shoulder to shoulder as a pastor with a worship pastor, or the worship pastor might answer to you. Whatever your situation, the relationship is critical."[16]

12. Miller, *Worship Leaders*, 12.
13. Miller, *Worship Leaders*, 12.
14. Miller, *Worship Leaders*, 59.
15. Wahl, "Most Important Relationship."
16. Fromm, "Critical Relationship."

5.4.2 Anecdotes and Personal Preferences

Currently, literature exploring the relationship of the tandem co-laboring in fruitful ministry is missing. There is anecdotal evidence and hypothesizing by various worship leaders and lead pastors in books and trade journals ranging from stating personal preferences, reflecting on their relationships, defining boundaries of the relationship, likening the relationship to a marriage, and common sense psychologizing practical usefulness. Personal preferences do not represent scholarly research, and research is absent on fruitful worship leading ministry.

This researcher's personal experience is that in 1987, the term, *worship leader*, was already in use at an independent Pentecostal church in Southern California, providing a parsonage to a husband-and-wife team who organized and led teams of musicians to lead the congregation in song. This singular observation evidences a specified and remunerated role. Although repetition of platitudes and anecdotes is only a starting point, these observations underscore the need to convey a realistic ministry experience and bring biblical clarity to the role.

5.4.3 Authoritative Research

Fortunately, Nelson Cowan writes authoritatively, "The term *worship leader*--designating a chief musician--circulated and arose organically in the late 1970s to early 1980s, especially among Pentecostals, as evident in the 1983 writings of Pentecostal author Judson Cornwall."[17] By using the biblical term, *chief musician*, Cowan dignifies the role, which introduces fifty-five Psalms in the King James Version. Chief Musician suggests something more than leading others in praise and worship around the campfire or a hootenanny.

---

17. Cowan, "Lay-Prophet-Priest," 24–31. Cowan refers to Cornwall, *Let us Worship*, 154.

One of the more prolific voices in training worship leaders is Vernon Whaley. He astutely assesses the twenty-first-century state of the role:

> The role of worship leader has become clearly defined over these last four or five decades. The demand has never been greater for thoroughly equipped, trained personnel to assume the pulpit and join the ranks as worship pastors. In fact, a recent research initiative by Liberty University's Center for Worship found that in 2018, there were no fewer than 5,650 job postings for a worship pastor. Most of these job postings are for full-time, trained, highly-skilled worship practitioners. The opportunities for worship leaders to serve the evangelical community encompass every church size and worship style imaginable–large, small, liturgical, free worship, charismatic, traditional, contemporary, multi-generational, multi-ethnic, praise, and worship, you name it.[18]

Whaley shows that the office has progressed over a half-century, into a role requiring extensive specialization. Thus, churches view this as a remunerated position, not limited to a particular branch of evangelical Christendom. He alternates the term, *worship leader*, with *worship pastor* and *worship practitioner*. One may presume this term shifting accommodates a wide variety of ecclesiastical settings. He does not attempt to date the term, but one reading may pin this to as early as 1968. As researchers studying worship leading as a field of inquiry, one may find an umbrella term—e.g., *Worship Leader* (with capitals) signifying a church office, even if there is no consensus on when the term, worship leader, came into the lexicon.

5.4.4 Challenges to Clarity

The New Testament leaves worship in the church open-ended. Ambiguity multiplies as the technology surrounding twenty-first-century worship advances so quickly—stretching the boundaries

18. Whaley, *Exalt His Name*, 85.

of the term to grope with the demands of the position. Technical specialization appears to be a significant reason lead pastors rely upon lead pastor-worship leaders. These situations highlight the necessity of identifying stable, biblical characteristics of what has worked in tandem that will prove helpful as it passes from one generation to the next (Ps 145:4; Eccl 1:4).

Finally, one comment from practical ministry leadership ends with this reminder: "Nevertheless, in a healthy church, our leadership always comes in second place to the leadership of the Holy Spirit working through everyone."[19] This third person is the Holy Spirit, the Spirit of Christ (Rom 8:9) in the phenomenon. Chuck Smith remained convinced by the Scriptures and through prayer that Jesus is the head of His church, and He would build His church (Matt 16:18). Leadership serves and stewards the body of Christ for the glory of God. With the working of the Holy Spirit and the Holy Scriptures as the final authority, Jesus Christ has graciously provided all that we need to build the Church in God's way.

5.4.5 Observations from Practitioners

Type in the search phrase, "Pastor Worship Leader relationship," in a search engine and well-intentioned advice returns from worship leaders, pastors, bloggers, or other self-proclaimed experts with varying degrees of experience. A sincere desire to help solve a problem or salve a painful relationship is the prevalent motive. These anecdotes intone empathy, speculating and offer common-sense solutions with Bible references attached in support.

5.4.5.1 General Observations from Protestants

The following extended quote from Dave DeSelm Ministries typifies the tenor of this anecdotal literature:

> The relationship between the senior Pastor and the worship leader is notorious for being frustrating and

---

19. Vaters, "Pastors and Worship Leaders."

distrustful on both sides . . . Whatever the reason . . . this partnership seems to get tested over and over again. It makes sense. These two individuals are responsible each week to lead people into the presence of God, to worship Him, hear from His Word, and allow it to change our lives. Our enemy, the devil, will do whatever he can to prevent that. And stirring up relational breakdown between the two key voices in the church has proven to be a winning strategy.[20]

The article is balanced—equally offering solutions, positively stated, to both persons in the relationship. He advises committing to a shared vision, clarifying roles, building trust, and finally acting quickly and privately to resolve misunderstandings and disagreements—biblical advice to work through a temporary snag. Nonetheless, ministering under a truce is not a biblical pattern for fruitful ministry.

Chuck Fromm, founder of *Worship Leader Magazine*, transcends the worship wars, by applying Scriptural principles from Jesus. Offering peace as a basis for a biblical, principled context to maintain unity and promote peace in the body of Christ, not by calling a truce.

> (Jesus) mediated the presence of God. He led in praying and answering questions about prayer. He sang psalms, hymns, and spiritual songs to God and led/joined others in doing so in the midst of corporate meetings and intimate fellowship . . . In addition to His example in scripture and our ongoing relationship with Him, Jesus left us with the Holy Spirit to not only reveal the heart of God *to* us but also to grow the heart of God *in* us.[21]

The ongoing relationship of mutual love found among Father, Son, and Holy Spirit is the model for a ministerial tandem to the body of Christ as an application of Jesus' teaching, "If a house be divided against itself, that house cannot stand" (Mark 3:25). The

20. DeSelm, "5 Relational Keys."
21. Fromm, "The Critical Relationship."

biblical principle of peace goes toward maintaining the unity of the Spirit in the bond of peace (Eph 4:3).

The in-tandem working relationship appears in Zac Hicks book, *The Worship Pastor,* notes the changing role of the twenty-first-century tandem as essential. "The pastor/worship leader relationship many times makes or breaks an effective ministry."[22] Hicks urges a worship leader to embrace the pastoral role and become a worship leader, not only an artist. His use of capital letters intends to broaden the specialized, multifaceted worship leader role from merely a performer or technician to further embrace the ecclesiastical role. This treatment addresses the worship leader side of the tandem and does not identify elements of a fruitful ministry.

5.4.5.2 General Observations From the Reformed Tradition

In a chapter entitled, "The Worship Leader and His Pastor,"[23] Worship Leader Andi Rozier reveals relational dynamics of the lead pastor/worship leader tandem and reoccurring themes of allegiance to and serving of the lead pastor as the lead worshipper. He alludes to the benefits of submission to the lead pastor from his experience serving with Pastor James MacDonald. Rozier describes MacDonald as "a passionate worshipper of Jesus Christ and frequently reminds our congregation that he preaches to make us all better worshippers."[24] In this tandem, the lead pastor leverages the ability of the worship leader to conduct the worship service.

Another dynamic lead pastor/worship leader ministry tandem is that of C. J. Mahaney and Bob Kauflin. The concluding two chapters of Kauflin's book, *Worship Matters,* advise each side of the lead pastor/worship leader tandem and what each can do to maintain the tandem relationship's unity. In a summary statement directed to the lead pastor, he writes: "God intends your relationship with your worship leader to be one of joy, mutual respect,

22. Hicks, *Worship Pastor,* 19.

23. Rozier, "Worship Leader and His Pastor," 141–52.

24. Rozier, *Doxology and Theology,* 142.

and fruitfulness. And with confidence in his Word, dependence on his Spirit, and reliance on the gospel, that's exactly what it will be."[25] The comment suggests a complementarity and gives insight into what the lead pastor/worship leader tandem does for the local church.

A pair of reciprocating articles written by a lead pastor[26] and a worship leader[27] Pappalardo and Passaro from the same church as a duet gives the other his perspective of an idealized ministry partner. This approach suggests complementarity and broadens the perspective of each. The two articles have twenty-six total suggestions so "that pastors and worship leaders can cultivate healthy relationships all for the sake of loving and leading the local church."[28]

5.2.5.3 A General Observation From the Spiritual Renewal Perspective

Author, worship leader, and senior pastor of Calvary Chapel, San Clemente, Holland Davis historically ties the collaborating tandem to nineteenth century revivalist movements.[29] He acknowledges a biblical context that shows the role derives from Ephesians 4:11–12 and 1 Corinthians 12:1–7 wherein the worship leader functions in the local church. He defines leading worship as a leadership function. "A worship leader is a pastor, teacher, prophet, evangelist, or apostle who is uniquely empowered by God to exercise their spiritual gifts through facilitating sung prayer."[30]

Davis goes onto state that the function is not primarily a musical or programming one, but worship leading is first a Spiritual act.[31] "It also means that I need to be in touch with the work of

25. Kauflin, *Worship Matters*, 258.

26. Greear, "What Every Pastor Wishes,"

27. Pappalardo and Passaro, "What Every Worship Leader."

28. Pappalardo and Passaro, "What Every Worship Leader."

29. Davis, *Let It Rise*, 54.

30. Davis, *Let It Rise*, 57.

31. Davis, *Let It Rise*, 59.

the Spirit within the community of believers I'm serving."[32] This view aligns with the spiritual renewal movement that began post-WWII and continues globally.

In nature, the fruit of the plant represents a mature plant that is capable of reproduction. Fruitful ministry suggests an ability to reproduce. Jesus taught that fruitfulness in ministry comes out of relationship of abiding in Christ (John 15:1–17). This teaching appears as a prime biblical example to replicate.

32. Davis, *Let It Rise*, 62.

6

Phenomenology for Christian Worship

CHRISTIAN WORSHIP REQUIRES MORE than just empirical observations. Observing the physical world to get at a spiritual reality is the difference between measuring a congregation singing to the ceiling, while the participants explain they are worshipping the living God. Apprehending the spiritual reality is more qualitative than quantitative. Objective discussion and analysis require a method suited to Christian worship that is more of spiritual exchange than performance. Thus, a phenomenological research method, design, and rationale—with the biblical worldview as its hermeneutical lens is necessary to provide qualitative data for the complex interactions involved in personal and congregational Christian worship leading.

It is quintessential to consider the lived experiences of pastors and worship leaders in fruitful ministry such as those working with Chuck Smith on Sunday Mornings at CCCM. By studying lived experiences to understand the phenomenon of worship leading in a fruitful ministry, the research necessitated the method. Phenomenology emerged over ethnography and narrative inquiry as most suitable to "define what is important—that is, *what needs to be studied* [emphasis original]"[1] since interactions, continuity, and situation are not present for narrative inquiry but are the products of phenomenology. This method possesses practical force for implementation. The final product anticipates a word picture of transcendent qualities of fruitfulness transcendent of any one ministry setting.

6.1 FORGING A WHOLISTIC PHENOMENOLOGY

Phenomenology requires a philosophical background. Christian worship requires a theological background. A researcher in Christian worship needs a standard of objectivity to *wholistically* examine the phenomenon in the physical and metaphysical domains. Twentieth-century Christian thinker Francis Schaeffer employed epistemological necessity when analyzing propositions.[2] He wrote, "The Bible teaches in two different ways: first, it teaches certain things in didactic statements . . . Second, the Bible teaches by showing how God works in the world that He Himself made . . . When I read the Bible, I find the infinite-personal God Himself works in history and the cosmos."

The hermeneutic phenomenological method with a biblical worldview lens then is a suitable *wholistic* method. The spiritual and material dimensions exist in an open system, where God is creator and enters into His creation. *Wholism* is the fuller sense that a biblical worldview apprehends. Thus, a basis for our being in both dimensions as one world—the whole world—is possible. The method, at minimum, does not disallow the possibility of the *wholistic* world. Hegel and Heidegger as phenomenologists permit this possibility, and yet, they subsequently focused on the materialistic.

The possibility becomes a rational pursuit of God. Christian worship demands this wider vision. Christian commentator Eric Metaxas writes, "God commands us to passionately and utterly

---

1. Leedy and Ormrod, *Practical Research*, 228.
2. Schaeffer, *Francis Schaeffer Trilogy*, 334.

and wholeheartedly *love* Him [emphasis original]."[3] Worship Leaders move and have their being in more than a merely empirical world. The congregations they lead evidence that "God is Spirit, and those who worship him must worship in Spirit and in truth" (John 4:24). Pastor Chuck Smith acknowledged the biblical worldview gives access to "the fact of complete and absolute truth, or 'true truth' as Francis Schaeffer calls it."[4]

6.2 RATIONALE FOR THE BIBLICAL WORLDVIEW AS HERMENEUTIC LENS

Norman L. Geisler's *Twelve Points that Show Christianity is True* logically demonstrates a sound rationale for using the biblical worldview as a hermeneutic lens. For example, the statement, "There is no propositional truth," asserts a propositional truth. Geisler defines truth as "what corresponds to reality. Truth matches its object."[5] This line of argumentation dismisses total skepticism and agnosticism, for the skeptic "is not skeptical about his skepticism"[6] and the agnostic knows enough to claim reality cannot be known. These propositions logically fail because they negate what they assert.

In Geisler's second chapter on logic, "Opposites Cannot Both Be True," he reviews three basic rules of thought: The Law of Identity, where A is A. The Law of Non-Contradiction, where A is not non-A. Finally explained is the Law of the Excluded Middle, where either A or non-A but not both. These self-evident truths have formidable consequences from the standpoint of rational thought. "For example, *If it is true that God exists, then it is false that God does not exist. If theism is true, then atheism is false (and vice versa).* Likewise, *If it is true that God does not exist, then theism is false*

3. Metaxas, *Letter to the American Church*.
4. Smith and Nixon, *Line Upon Line*, 10.
5. Geisler, *Twelve Points*, 5.
6. Geisler, *Twelve Points*, 5.

that God does exist. If atheism is true, then theism is false."[7] The examples illustrate that contradictions cannot be true at the same time and in the same way.

An important consideration following from the Law of Non-Contradiction is that one religion from a purely logical perspective could be true. "Either God exists, or He does not. And if it is false that God does not exist, then it is true that God does exist." Geisler, in illustrating how logic applies, is not trying to prove any particular religion.

From these first two chapters, Geisler builds the case throughout the rest of the book to show a theistic God exists, because the other views are either inconsistent or contradictory. Then he shows that miracles are possible because the miracle of creation—something from nothing—has already happened. Then, he asserts that miracles performed in connection with a truth claim confirm the truth of God through a messenger of God. "Making predictions that come to pass in advance of the event gives even more certainty that it is of God."[8]

From these points/chapters, Geisler continues toward specificity. A sixth point is that the historicity of the New Testament documents is reliable through multiple lines of evidence and exceed a rigorous standard for acceptance far beyond any other ancient manuscripts. Geisler's chapter seven asserts that from eyewitnesses in the New Testament, Jesus claimed to be God. His following chapter argues convincingly that Jesus' claim to be God was proven by a unique convergence of miracles that show Jesus supernaturally fulfilled dozens of Old Testament predictive events including his prediction of his own death, burial, and resurrection. Chapter nine then briefly goes on to say, "The central claim of Christianity is true and opposing claims are false."[9] Jesus' claim to be God was confirmed from God in human flesh.

The final three chapters give the rationale for the use of the biblical worldview as a hermeneutic lens. Chapter ten shows that

7. Geisler, *Twelve Points*, 9.

8. Geisler, *Twelve Points*, 43.

9. Geisler, *Twelve Points*, 106.

whatever Jesus affirmed as true, is true. "So, even what Jesus taught as a human being, was absolutely true. He not only was "the truth" (John 14:6), but everything he spoke was the truth. He never uttered any errors. As the son of God, He could not. And as the son of Mary, He did not. He was both divine and human, but never erred as either."[10]

Chapter eleven shows that in the New Testament Jesus affirmed that the Bible is the word of God. His final chapter concludes, "Christianity (in its essential teachings) is true, and whatever is opposed to any of these teachings is false. In short, Christianity is the true religion, and any other religion that opposes its core teachings is a false religion as such, regardless of whatever other truths it may contain."[11] Thus, the rationale is for the biblical worldview to be embraced as a hermeneutic lens.

6.3 GUIDING DOCUMENTS

Two twenty-first-century published works contextualize and format this research. First is Charles E. Fromm's case study, "Textual Communities and New Song in the Multimedia Age: The Routinization of Charisma in the Jesus Movement."[12] A case study provides essential background to learn more about "a little-known or poorly understood situation."[13] Fromm's familiarity with the Smiths, the movement, and his extensive experience in publishing, all serve as starting points for his inquiry and advance research. The second guiding document was Katarzyna Peoples' *How to Write a Phenomenological Dissertation*.[14] Peoples insists that making explicit biases is essential within hermeneutic phenomenology.[15]

---

10. Geisler, *Twelve Points*, 110.

11. Geisler, *Twelve Points*, 123.

12. Fromm, "Textual Communities."

13. Leedy, Ormond, and Johnson, *Practical Research*, 231.

14. Peoples, *Phenomenological Dissertation*.

15. Peoples, *Phenomenological Dissertation*, 34.

A guiding document for explicating the data is Chuck Smith's *Calvary Chapel Distinctives*. This book gave the participants the central advantage of including Smith in the study. Although deceased, Smith remains a participant through his teaching of Scripture and his written works that were common to all the participants.

The Bible is the primary document guiding communication of the data. A biblical worldview lens focuses to understand an unseen phenomenon. Furthermore, all the participants minister in accordance with a biblical worldview providing a common lexicon and contextual narrative space for obtaining qualitative data through interviews.

6.4 METHODOLOGICAL SUMMARY

This phenomenological study with the biblical worldview as hermeneutic lens advances a method sufficient to observe the Christian engaged in worship. Jesus taught if anyone wants to do God's will, that one will know by testing and through experience whether the teaching is from God. And yet, if one acts on their own authority that person desires self-honor and not God (John 7:17–18). God's ongoing invitation into a relationship with God, received by many hippies, found peace and love was found through the Prince of Peace (Isa 9:6) and the God of love (2 Cor 13:11) in the Bible. God's invitation remains open to true seekers of truth today. Scripture can be tested and verified, as in the old adage, "The proof of the pudding is in the eating." Psalm 34:8 NET invites the attentive to "Taste and see that the Lord is good! How blessed is the person who trusts in him!"

6.4.1 Instrumentation

Interviews were the primary instrument to gather the participants data about their direct experiences in the fruitful ministry of CCCM on Sunday mornings. Interviewing captured the phenomenon of worship leading in fruitful ministry as the worship leader led in tandem with Chuck Smith on Sunday Mornings at CCCM. This focus on experiences informs the conveyance of the phenomenon and is essential to avoid indirect methods of investigation.[16]

A twenty-question survey and other extant data were used to create a biographical sketch of the participants for this project. This historical frame of reference was a point of entry on the hermeneutic circle to assist the researcher's understanding of the lived experiences from the interviews. Interviews were a second point to begin movement along the hermeneutic circle. Peoples describes a process of constant revision, where "understanding increases by moving from the understanding of parts to the understanding of the whole and back again to the parts, continually changing as new data are introduced."[17] These points of entry onto the circle are thus established.

6.4.2 Data Collection

Each round of interviews was generated by the author from the individual's research data and began to form a composite conception of the group's shared lived experiences. The aim was to uncover any common attributes, characteristics, and themes to saturate the phenomenon. The research sought understanding of these worship leaders' lived experiences collaborating in tandem with Chuck Smith in fruitful ministry on Sunday mornings to reveal and communicate essential elements of fruitful ministry. The focused attention on this complex phenomenon, as experienced, informs Christian worship in significant ways. The biblical worldview asserts that God's reason for creating humans in His own image is so that His glory is magnified by willing, autonomous beings who commune and enjoy fellowship in a personal relationship with God, characterized by His love. Worship of the

---

16. Peoples, *Dissertation Guide*, 51.
17. Peoples, *Dissertation Guide*, 33.

true and living God is quite literally the human *raison d'être* (Psalm 16:5, 119:57, 142:5, 142:5)

The data consisted of participant interviews, extant literature, and the journaling product of the researcher while mentally traveling within the participants' experiences around the hermeneutic circle. Phenomenologist Victor Gijbers defines the hermeneutic circle as "a process of interpretation in which we continually move between smaller and larger units of meaning in order to determine the meaning of both."[18] The interview, to collect data, reflexivity in thinking and journaling are keys to phenomenological methodology.[19] The method generated questions that would slightly diverge among participants' responses to verify the extent of the group's experiences.

The interviews were video-recorded online and stored on a password-protected computer. Each interview took about an hour to complete. Each participant was granted three interviews, in a semi-structured interview format.

These dimensions of authenticity, explicated biblically, formed a stable pattern of service for the lead pastor/worship leader tandem that tests the thesis and forms the biblical essence of fruitful ministry for replication in a globally networked church context to flourish.

6.4.3 Explication of Data

Explication replaces the phrase, "data analysis" (for quantitative inquiry), to describe the chore of unfolding a phenomenon for generating greater meaning by traveling around the hermeneutic circle. The researcher sought to saturate and understand the phenomenon by breaking down interview data of participants' lived experiences into smaller meaning units—all the while keeping the context of the whole in view where all the units of relevant

---

18. Gijbers, "Chapter 4.1."
19. Peoples, *Dissertation Guide*, 52.

meaning are returned clustered together.[20] For cohesion of data, it is noted that participants and researcher share a biblical worldview and an inerrant view of Scripture.

Explication unfolded through the biblical worldview of worship leaders, which provided a pre-existing and common lexicon relied upon, but not presumed upon, in this constant revisionary process of understanding. "Since the goal of phenomenological research is to illuminate the lived experience(s) of a phenomenon, the method of data analysis is emergent."[21]

Paradoxically, the objectivity of explication was achieved by the interpretation of subjective data, in transcribing interviews, delineating units of meaning, identifying possible standard relevant units, clustering units of relevant meaning, determining themes, and composing a summative contextualization.[22] The over-arching culmination of the project was to conceptually and fairly examine experiential data to better understand the phenomenon.

6.5 METHODOLOGICAL IMPLICATIONS

In the Bible, there is reliable evidence emanating from God's words, his works, and rational human thought to reasonably establish the God of theism. Geisler notes, "Distinct from all other views of God since there can only be one indivisible, infinite, necessary, absolutely perfect Uncaused Cause of everything else that exists . . . the viability of this precondition of evangelical theology is well supported by numerous lines of evidence."[23] Thus, God's worth is established with incomparable value and is inherently present since God's existence is necessary, and humanity's existence is contingent upon God.

Theology has shown that God's existence is necessarily true, and many aspects of God's existence are knowable. In worship,

20. Hycner, "Some Guidelines," 281.
21. Peoples, *Dissertation Guide*, 58.
22. Hycner, "Some Guidelines," 282.
23. Geisler *Systematic Theology*, 33.

contingent beings find themselves ascribing worth to God's state of necessary being—a contrast between finite and infinite that sets the foundation and basis of worship. God has created man after His image (Gen 1:26; Ps 17:15; Rom 6:5; Phil 2:7). God and humanity have, at minimum, the capacity to engage in some form of discourse. Since God is the source of everything and communication with God is possible, it is conceivable to enjoy communication with God.

Each Sunday, leaders of worship (including pastors) implement a practical theology of worship. A positive correlation is presumed between human understanding and God's self-revelation. Jesus corrected the woman at the well: "Ye worship ye know not what: we know what we worship: for salvation is of the Jews" (John 4:22) and instructs, "that they that worship him must worship him in spirit and in truth" (John 4:23).

7

The Wholistic Phenomenon of Christian Worship

THE RESEARCH FINDINGS PRESENTED in this chapter connect the hermeneutical phenomenology method with the biblical worldview as its interpretive lens. Chuck Smith taught, "We discover truth by what God has revealed to us through His Word and the testimony of the Holy Spirit, as well as observed facts of God's created order. Therefore, truth is knowable because God has revealed it to us."[1] The biblical understanding among the participants provides a communicative basis for the participants' lived experiences and allows the possibility of coherence for saturation. The participants' data is thematically situated around the values described in *The Calvary Chapel Distinctives.*[2]

7.1 A FRUITFUL ENVIRONMENT

Donald E. Miller posited, "Chuck Smith displays the prototypical style of leadership for new paradigm churches."[3] Smith's values in

---

1. Smith and Nixon, *Line Upon Line,* 11.

2. Smith, *Calvary Chapel Distinctives.*

3. Miller, *Reinventing,* 139.

the *Distinctives* frame the interactions. One biblical example that may guide a textual community regarding the verbal communicative interactions (speaking and singing) is inherent in Paul's admonition to the Colossians: "Let the word of Christ dwell in you richly in all wisdom; teaching and admonishing one another in psalms and hymns and spiritual songs, singing with grace in your hearts to the Lord" (Col 3:16). The obedience of faith regulates these interactions.[4] Sunday morning services at CCCM employ congregational singing as a practical implementation of Colossians 3:16, but with an array of forms. Theologian Grudem's remarks reflects upon how congregations apply the biblical text in their liturgies:

> Evangelicals need . . . not too quickly dismiss unfamiliar forms of worship: people in liturgical churches should realize that spontaneity can be managed in an orderly way, and people in charismatic groups should realize that edification and genuine worship can occur within a detailed structure . . . Yet any one form that is used excessively can become a meaningless routine for most participants.[5]

At least one charismatic interpreter serving the congregation facilitated the interactions. Pastor Smith (as both lead pastor and worship leader) served as charismatic interpreter.

7.2 THEMES AND VALUES

Calvary Chapel Costa Mesa's ministry approach that led to its success and fruitful significance is based around thirteen biblically-derived values. The phenomenon of fruitful ministry occurred—not magically—but because of the biblical values communicated by Smith to extend the ministry's influence. The thirteen values (also headings in this chapter) are as follows: (1) The Call to Ministry, (2) God's Model for the Church, (3) Church Government: Jesus is

---

4. The phrase, "obedience to the faith," opens Romans 1:5 and is a key phrase in the closing doxology of Romans 16:26. This concept bookends the epistle that regulates Christian conduct of Jews and gentiles.

5. Grudem, *Systematic Theology*, footnote 1012.

Head of the Church, (4) The Born-Again Experience; (5) Building the Church God's Way, (6) Grace Upon Grace, (7) The Priority of The Word, (8) The Centrality of Christ, (9) The Rapture of the Church, (10) Having Begun in the Spirit, (11) The Supremacy of Love is Objective Evidence of The Spirit, (12) Striking the Balance, and (13) Ventures of Faith.

7.2.1 The Call to Ministry

After the "Preface" of the *Distinctives* is a zero chapter, "The Call to Ministry." Smith believed, "If there is one characteristic that is absolutely essential for effective ministry, it's that we must first have a sense of calling—the conviction in our hearts that God has chosen and called us to serve Him."[6] All participants recall experiencing their calling into worship leading.

One survey question was, "When did you first sense you were called into music?" The question was intended to determine a sequence of events. The researcher's fore-conception was that first one was a music-lover, then at some later point in life, they were born-again, and subsequently, they were called into music ministry. The word, "called," was taken by these worship leaders not in a general affinity to music but refers to this specific call into ministry. The fore-conception was revised and the participant experiences revealed an important quality of fruitful ministry.

They unanimously understood the word, call, in the sense of Smith's strong conviction from God—a call to ministry. In the mind of the researcher, a natural connection with music would have been as though they had heard the call of music in a general sense that preceded salvation. This was the intention behind the question, but their sense of calling was specific and strong. None interpreted *called* in the general way that the researcher had posed the question. In the interviews, the general sense of liking music preceded being born-again. Their unanimous and more narrow interpretation of called stems from Rom 8:28–30 and leads one to

6. Smith, *Calvary Chapel Distinctives*, 3.

maintain this intense sense of conviction of calling is essential to fruitful worship ministry.

A related fore-conception of the researcher was that there would inevitably be a period wherein the individual would report experiencing a dilemma surrounding the nuances between the experience of being a musician who became a Christian and being a Christian musician. The fore-conception was that being set apart for God's service would conflict with secular music. For the nascent musicians, the learning music phase melded with becoming a born-again Christian musician and was merely one more experience on their life journey to integrate into their being.

Those who had been performers "in the world" (before becoming a born-again believer) report an adjustment time where the new believer stopped performing publicly for two reasons. One reason was the fear of being drawn away from their new relationship with Jesus into their former life of sin. The second reason was that they sensed that they had the liberty to play music, but it was not expedient for their spiritual growth as a new Christian. They had offered their whole being to God. The God who is there had only asked for a pause for them to nurture their relationship with Him. They practiced and played privately but did not perform publicly. God eventually consecrated their musical ability redeeming it for His service.

Another survey item asks, "Please list years involved in leading worship all churches and settings." Three of the five participants at the time of writing are currently leading worship in churches. Some only mentioned churches on the survey, though, in the interviews, all engaged in worship-leading experiences outside of church. Taking the written responses from the survey only and rounding to whole years, the range of years leading is 28–49 years, the median is thirty-three years, and the mean greater than thirty-six years. These worship leaders are life-long worshippers. It is more than a service they perform; it is who they are as Christians, their master status.[7]

7. Knox, *Sociology is Rude*, 58.

A more specific item asks, "Please list any other churches where you led worship in Sunday morning services." All worship leaders led worship in other churches and settings before coming to CCCM. Three other survey items: "Have you ever been involved in musical outreaches?" and "Have you any published works?" and "Do you have a personal Bible reading plan?" all yielded unanimous yes responses.

7.2.2 God's Model for the Church

Chapter one of the *Distinctives* is "God's Model for the Church." The opening line reads, "In Calvary Chapel we look to the book of Acts as the model for the church."[8] The source of historicization is not a denominational founder or manifestations of spiritual gifts, but the Bible. Smith places Jesus Christ and the text of Scripture at the foundation and center of the church, exemplified by Jesus' quote: "I will build my church" (Matt 16:18). Smith links CCCM to first-century Jerusalem as the template that proves paradigmatic.

Smith summarizes the Acts church is ever-primitive, and ever-contemporary as is its founder and builder, "Jesus Christ the same yesterday, and today, and forever" (Heb 13:8). "The Word of God was the top priority in the ministry of the early church, along with prayer . . . When the church is what God intends the church to be, when the church is doing what God wants the church to do, then the Lord will do what He wants to do for the church. And He will add daily to the church those that should be saved."[9] The worship leaders appreciate the authenticity of the Acts church.

7.2.3 Church Government: Jesus is Head of the Church

Chapter 2 of the *Distinctives* is "Church Government" and concludes with, "The pastor is ruled by the Lord and aided by the Elders to discover the mind and will of Jesus Christ for His church.

8. Smith, *Calvary Chapel Distinctives*, 9.
9. Smith, *Calvary Chapel Distinctives*, 13.

This in turn is implemented by the Assistant Pastors."[10] Assistant pastors thus positioned set the form for the worship leader. Smith believed every believer was to serve the body of Christ. Staff was especially called and empowered to serve the body of Christ. The worship leader has an area of ministry (Rom 12:27), but every believer has the ministry of helps (1 Cor 12:28).

Smith's experience showed that titles set one person over another, and the scriptural position is that this should never be the case. "It is my belief that everyone should be a deacon. The ministry of helps was the essence of the deacon's function . . . they were to look after the congregation and help the sick."[11] Serving the liturgy to the congregation is a function within the role of the worship leader as a deacon. Smith's reasoning was such that everyone one is subject to Christ and the scriptures. Jesus as "servant of all" (Mark 9:35) set the basic ministry pattern. Smith was wary of giving out titles and offices as these tend to elevate one person above another. This practice can produce an effect which runs counter to that of servant leadership which Jesus inaugurated at John 13 with the menial task of foot washing (John 13:13–17).

From his first invitation as a guest speaker (and throughout his forty-eight years at CCCM), Smith led the Sunday morning service with congregational singing using the hymnbook synergistically to emphasize points from the Sunday morning teaching, expounding Scripture.[12] One worship leader explains Pastor Smith's practice: "Chuck would always choose that opening hymn that (Sunday) morning—it was the first thing he'd do. He'd . . . open the hymnal and choose the hymns that would speak into his message . . . we would do the same thing . . . arrange the worship songs accordingly to fit into what he was teaching as much as possible."[13] The desire to support the text is what Fromm notes as a hallmark of a worship leader who also was a charismatic interpreter.

10. Smith, *Distinctives*, 26.

11. Smith, *Distinctives*, 23.

12. Fromm, "Textual Communities," 145.

13. Participant, interview.

7.2.4 The Born-Again Experience

Pastor Smith, in chapter three of the *Distinctives*—"Empowered By The Spirit"—states, "We acknowledge a three-fold relationship between the Holy Spirit and the believer represented by three Greek prepositions—'*para*,' '*en*,' and '*epi*.'"[14] The Greek prepositions are listed in order of increasing intimacy in relationship with Christ. *Para* translates "with." The Holy Spirit is *para* with every person prior to conversion and is the convicting work of the Holy Spirit as Jesus teaches in John 16:7–15. *En* translates to "in." Jesus distinguishes these in one verse, "The Spirit of truth; whom the world cannot receive, because it seeth him not, neither knoweth him: but ye know him; for he dwelleth with [*Para*] you and shall be in [*En*] you" (John 14:17).

The Greek preposition *epi*—often translated in the New Testament as "upon" or "over" is a subsequent work of the Holy Spirit overflowing the life of a born-again believer distinct from the subjective work of the Holy Spirit in the first two relationships. The overflow is an observable manifestation of the Spirit, which "allows the Holy Spirit to flow forth out of our lives. Our lives then are not just a vessel containing the Spirit, but they become channels by which the Spirit flows forth to touch the world around us. I also believe that this is the objective work of the Spirit."[15] All the worship leaders acknowledge a born-again experience.

For fruitful ministry, Smith interpreted Jesus's teaching on fruitfulness that as the branches draw life and produce fruit by remaining connected to the true vine, so do disciples in Christ bear fruit (John 15:1–17). Smith teaches this *epi*—overflowing of the Spirit is the ultimate human experience "only for those who allow God to bring forth much fruit in their lives."[16] He also warns, "God isn't looking for the works of our flesh. God wants the fruit that sprouts from our lives because of our vital relationship with

---

14. Smith, *Calvary Chapel Distinctives*, 28–29.
15. Smith, *Calvary Chapel Distinctives* 29.
16. Smith, *Living Water*, 290.

Him."[17] He draws out the analogy, "Just as branch draws its nourishment and energy from the vine so do you from the Spirit. It is through the Spirit that God's life flows through you."[18] A relationship with Christ and the subsequent faith journey of walking in the Spirit after initial justification is essential.

7.2.5 Building the Church God's Way

In chapter four, Chuck Smith shares, "We are of the belief that *if the Lord doesn't build the house, they labor in vain who build it.*"[19] Casual[20] and relaxed[21] are common descriptions for the style of ministry at CCCM.

Sociological and historical observers have attributed the Southern California lifestyle[22] to explain why the ministry style has been successful. Still others offering a psychological understanding note Smith's personality[23] as the source for the style and philosophy of ministry. With the biblical lens, neither viewpoint is true to the situation. Smith says, "If we have complete confidence that it's His church, that He's going to build it, and that He's going to do His job, then all I have to do is be faithful."[24] Smith then warns the leadership, "If you try to carry the burden and the load . . . you'll find yourself under pressure . . . then you begin to push and manipulate people. That isn't the Calvary Chapel style."[25]

The standard is that Jesus is the head of the Church and God produces results through the working of the Holy Spirit according to God's inspired word. Therefore, hype and programs are out

17. Smith, *Living Water,* 290.

18. Smith, *Living Water,* 291.

19. Smith, *Distinctives.* The italicized text is Smith's emphasis and is an excerpt from Psalm 127:1, 33.

20. Miller, *Reinventing,* 31–32.

21. Miller, *Reinventing,* 79.

22. Balmer, *Mine Eyes Have Seen,* chapter one.

23. Efron, "Calvary Chapel Stands."

24. Smith, *Calvary Chapel Distinctives,* 33.

25. Smith, *Calvary Chapel Distinctives,* 33–34.

in favor of allowing people to freely worship God. Keeping the congregational attention on exalting Christ and focusing human attention on what the Holy Spirit was doing on Sunday mornings, biblically guided, underpins what was done and not done.

Worship leaders did not always understand the reason *why* things were done, though they clearly knew *what* to do or not do. One worship leader revealed a limiting direction from Smith: "I remember being directed once to not 'cheerlead.' He didn't want me to prompt people."[26] The worship leader is not to conduct a response but allow people to respond in worship, authentically. This does not imply that anything goes. Directing the congregation's response to God's presence is out and yet maintaining the setting "as unto the Lord" is important for continuity. Programming a worship response is inauthentic.

Fromm recognized the importance of rituals for a textual community—"not only for transmission of information, but for the transformation of lives."[27] Spiritually vibrant rituals "must be continually revised and reinvented by the communities' charismatic interpreters."[28] For rituals to remain vital, they must serve the textual community by supplying structure for interactions vertical (God-to-individual, individual-to God) as well as horizontal (among the congregation). Congregational singing and responsive scripture reading are ancient rituals, but they rely upon the Holy Spirit to reinfuse them with a fresh work of the Spirit.

Congregants must not be cajoled or worked up by the charismatic interpreter. "Shared religious belief is a powerful basis for spiritual kinship, but beliefs remain inside people's minds until they are expressed outwardly in symbolic actions that build identification."[29] The Holy Spirit inspired the biblical text has also outlined how Holy Spirit manifests during the Sunday morning service.

---

26. Participant, interview.
27. Fromm, "Textual Communities," 344.
28. Fromm, "Textual Communities," 344.
29. Fromm, "Textual Communities," 343.

The human ministers merely created space for the Holy Spirit to minister in the Sunday morning service. Smith saw his ministry, out of necessity, as all that could be carried out, given the existence of a mixed multitude (born-again and others). People want to be a part of anything significant that God wants to do. A mixed multitude accumulates around a move of God the way people gather around a house on fire and explains why police departments have the yellow tape to keep onlookers from getting involved. Yet, a Christian worship service, conducted publicly, must not keep onlookers out and standing back. They are welcomed to witness the objective working of the Holy Spirit as the overflow of the born-again believer.

7.2.6 Grace Upon Grace

In chapter five of *Distinctives*, Smith reminds the reader, "We need the grace of God in our lives . . . daily. We experience it, and we're saved by it personally. But we also stand in grace. We believe in the love and grace that seeks to restore the fallen."[30] The worship leaders associated grace with what God has done and as an example for the Christian to live; "forgiveness,"[31] "kindness,"[32] "loving,"[33] and by simply asking, "How can I help?"[34] One worship leader recalled a line from his reflections interacting with Smith. "Methods are many, principles are few. The methods always change, the principles never do. He was really gracious with all that."[35]

Smith admits, "I have taken chances, brought fellows on staff who had supposedly repented and later on, the same trials were still there. And I will probably make mistakes in the future. But I will tell you this, if I'm going to err, I want to err on the side of grace

---

30. Smith, *Calvary Chapel Distinctives*, 41.
31. Participant, interview.
32. Participant, interview.
33. Participant, interview.
34. Participant, interview.
35. Participant, interview.

rather than on the side of judgment."[36] His view is that to hold too tightly to either side of a divisive issue is less important than to teach all that God's word says about it with an open hand. Smith admonishes, "Let us always be certain to look at the fruit of the teaching."[37] This implies that the fruit of the Spirit is love (Gal 5:22).

7.2.7 The Priority of the Word

Chapter six of the *Distinctives* states, "Another primary distinctive of Calvary Chapel is our endeavor to declare the whole counsel of God."[38] Pastor Smith again points to Acts 20:27–28 when Paul speaks to the Ephesian elders. Rhetorically, Smith asks, how can someone make this claim to declare the whole counsel of God today unless the teacher takes a congregation from Genesis to Revelation?

As this project shows, a biblical worldview is essential for ministry at CCCM as well as for the study of the phenomenon. The worship leaders as members of the textual community both hear and apply the biblical text. On Sunday nights, Smith led the congregation through every verse of the entire Bible, "*lectio continua,*"[39] at least eight times from Genesis to Revelation.

7.2.8 The Centrality of Christ

Chapter seven of the *Distinctives* was originally a central feature of CCCM to distance itself from its Pentecostal roots. "One of the important characteristics is the centrality of Jesus Christ in our worship. We don't allow any practice or behavior that would distract people from focusing on Him . . . When distractions do take place, deal with them and if necessary, publicly talk about them."[40] Visual

---

36. Smith, *Calvary Chapel Distinctives,* 47.

37. Smith, *Calvinism,* 16.

38. Smith, *Distinctives,* 51.

39. Fromm, "Textual Communities," 154.

40. Smith, *Distinctives,* 57, 60.

distractions were limited. Standing and waving hands distracts. All worship leaders mentioned the service was designed to limit even the potential for distraction and be very time efficient. Smith was "adamant on reducing distraction in church.[41]

Smith insisted congregational singing begin with a familiar song. Introduce new songs, either second, or best, as the last song where the worship leader would have everyone sit to learn the new song. If everyone was standing during the third song, they were to have the congregation sit down. This was to have the congregation rise in reverence to participate in the responsive reading ritual of the worship service wherein a pastor reads the odd-numbered verses of a passage, and the congregation responds by reading the even verses.

These practices apply variably across affiliated churches, though the principle to keep the attention on Christ is upheld. Some churches have everyone stand together at the opening song and then be seated at personal discretion. Some teach that since a variety of postures appear in scripture, variety is permitted in the congregation. Some are comfortable with standing or kneeling but only in the back of the church. Some permit reverent kneeling up front. The variability in worship postures may be a result of the Calvary Chapel style of worship, which has impacted culture, generally. Many scholars have suggested that Renewalists have changed worship in the twenty-first century.

Since WWII (and consonant with second wave spiritual renewal movements), one's posture during worship became more expressive leading to a wider range of acceptable forms. There has been a shift in personal deportment in congregational worship as charismatic expressions of faith behaviors once associated with spiritual grandstanding and considered inauthentic responses to the divine presence are now more the norm. For example, the posture of standing with arms raised in surrender or in spiritual impoverishment has become a culturally acceptable response to the divine presence and not self-aggrandizement.

---

41. Participant, interview.

Smith valued authentic whole-hearted worship. The worship leaders noted this and how today it is not strictly connected with first wave Pentecostal worship. Smith supported worship but would not exalt an individual. Smith reminded, "That no flesh should glory in His presence" (1 Cor 1:29).

7.2.9 The Rapture of the Church

In *Distinctives*, chapter eight's "The Rapture of the Church" is twice as long as any other chapter. With its prominent focus in the chapter, the Rapture represents an important aspect of fruitful ministry. Smith holds the pre-tribulation rapture is essential for fruitful ministry. "I believe your view of the Rapture will have a significant impact on the success on your ministry."[42] For biblical and practical reasons, the believer is influenced by holding this view of eschatology. At the time of this writing, none of the worship leaders opposed the doctrine of the pre-tribulation Rapture of the church. Since their time of service with Smith, two worship leaders have revised their position to be more accepting of alternate views.

One worship leader voiced the majority view: "The imminent return of Jesus is a central . . . one of the most important theological positions of Calvary Chapel. It's one of the main distinctives because it makes the worship more important, because it kind of fuels mission and evangelism."[43] Three worship leaders agree that the imminent return of Christ and the pre-tribulation Rapture of the Church is where the preponderance of the biblical evidence points. Without an imminent return, the Christian would look for the coming of Anti-Christ as a sign of the times to gain an accurate idea of the return of Christ, which would render needless Jesus' repeated warnings to watch and be ready.

Smith developed an authoritative position from Scripture after thorough study of the various human interpretations. Smith states, "There are many pastors who claim an ignorance of the

42. Smith, *Calvary Chapel Distinctives*, 65.

43. Participant interview.

Rapture or say that they are not certain whether it will precede the Tribulation . . . We have our Bibles, and we're capable of studying this subject thoroughly."[44] Considering that CCCM's ministry is paradigmatic and arguably the most fruitful ministry model of the twentieth century, this distinctive deserves careful examination and thorough study.

Miller sees this view as a strength of new paradigm churches as centers to restore hope:

> For many people in this country there is a "hope deficit," to which new paradigm churches are responding. People need not only healing of specific problems but also a sense of destiny, a conviction that their lives have purpose and meaning. New paradigm churches are particularly effective at projecting hope (sometimes in rather millennial terms) and joy. In content this may be the "old-time religion," but in spirit it addresses the fundamental need for ecstasy, which consumerism does not supply.[45]

It is outside the scope of the study to quantify the projected hope that results from believing in the Rapture of the church. Nevertheless, the imperative in Jesus' teaching is to be fruitful. Clearly, in John 15:1–17, the command is to produce fruit in ministry. Furthermore, Jesus taught to judge from the point of view that a tree is known is by its fruit (Matt 7:20). History affirms that CCCM's pretribulation-rapture position has produced fruit, fruit that remains, and hope.

The Rapture position has biblical and practical implications. It produces an interpretive framework of the biblical text and a ministry imperative that Smith identified as essential to fruitfulness. Holding this position has led to 1000s of churches and ministries around the word proclaiming the gospel. The fruit is that the Spirit of Christ has entered into the lives of millions of the converted. Fromm says, "Dramatic events in world history were of seminal importance in galvanizing the Calvary Chapel congregation . . .

44. Smith, *Calvary Chapel Distinctives*, 65.

45. Miller, *Reinventing*, 185.

with a sense of the imminence of prophetic fulfillment and a corollary sense of urgency of missionary work in the "last days."'"[46]

7.2.10 Having Begun in the Spirit

Pastor Smith leads chapter nine of the *Distinctives* by explaining, "Calvary Chapel is a work that was begun by the Spirit. Every new and great movement of God is born of the Spirit . . . Yet such moves of the Spirit historically seem to move from that birth in the Spirit to ultimately seeking to be perfected in the flesh . . . a continual cycle."[47] Drawing upon Paul's imperative at Galatians 5:25 that Smith wishes to impart, he emphasizes in bold—"Having begun in the Spirit, let us continue in the Spirit!"[48] This value is one where all the worship leaders see themselves holding to as they continue in ministry. Fromm anchors the phenomenon: "As converts whose souls have been lit on fire with the flame of the Spirit, we will have our own story to tell; we become not just consumers of the message, but producers."[49] As charismatic interpreters of the inspired texts, these worship leaders are moved by the same Spirit as the text (2 Pet 1:21).

7.2.11 The Supremacy of Love is Objective Evidence of the Spirit

In chapter ten of the *Distinctives*, Smith makes two sweeping statements that result from his relationship with God and from over fifty years of experience serving the Lord. The first is "God's supreme desire for us is that we experience His love and then share that love with others."[50] Love is first communicated on the vertical axis from God-to-human. This love reciprocates in worship from

46. Fromm, "Textual Communities," 167.

47. Smith, *Calvary Chapel Distinctives,* 89.

48. Smith, *Calvary Chapel Distinctives,* 96.

49. Fromm, "Textual Communities," 355.

50. Smith, *Calvary Chapel Distinctives* 102.

human to God. One result is then that Christian love communicates horizontally human-to-human.

The second statement moderates the horizontal relationships among believers in Christ. "I've come to the conclusion that its more important that I have the right attitude than that I have the right answers . . . Better that we have the right attitude and the wrong answers, than the right answers with the wrong attitude. Remember that the next time you get into an argument . . . over some doctrinal position or issue."[51] The worship leaders pattern their ministry after Smith's teaching that this quality of love is the objective manifestation of the Holy Spirit in the born-again life.

7.2.12 Striking the Balance

Chapter eleven in the *Distinctives* states,

> An important characteristic of Calvary Chapel Fellowships is our desire not to divide God's people over non-essential issues. This is not to say that we do not have strong convictions. When the Bible speaks clearly, we must as well. But on other issues we try to recognize the Scriptural validity of both sides of a debate and avoid excluding or favoring."[52]

This value may explain why no worship leader opposed the pre-tribulation Rapture issue although today some are reluctant to hold that view to the exclusion of the other views. On that issue, CCCM (with Smith) taught that there is sufficient biblical data to arrive at that conclusion. Given Jesus' commands to watch[53] and be ready, and its inherent power to drive ministry, it is essential. Currently, two participants choose to leave it open-ended. Even when there is disagreement among the leadership, there is reluctance to divide God's people.

51. Smith, *Calvary Chapel Distinctives*, 102.
52. Smith, *Calvary Chapel Distinctives*, 107.
53. Matthew 25:13; Mark 13:37; Luke 21:36, and others.

Holland Davis is a participant of the study and as a public figure, he consented to using his name. As a worship leader for fifty years, He is also lead pastor of Calvary Chapel San Clemente, since 2010. Working from both sides of the lead pastor/worship leader interaction, he provides perspective to upholding the Pre-tribulation rapture position. "As a Bible teacher, I began to look at the text for myself. My views changed just from the scriptures—not reading books. just reading the scriptures."[54]

This point that the biblical text anchors a textual community is the dividing point between Vineyard and Calvary (Davis has also served as worship leader in both the Vineyard and Calvary movements). This is also the distinctive point between the second and third waves of Pentecostalism as discussed, previously. Fromm explains the formal parting of ways stemmed from a 1982 planning meeting for Calvary Chapel's annual pastors conference.[55] "The underlying issue was the text: who or what was at the center of the community? How was charisma to be contained?"[56]

In striking the balance, no parting of the ways was necessary so long as John Wimber, Pastor of Calvary Chapel Yorba Linda, and the leading authority representing what would become the Vineyard movement, return to centering the community on teaching the Word of God.[57] His "authority had become self-referential and self-determining. Wimber was now standing in the authority of the prophet."[58] The *Third Wave of Pentecostalism* begins with its challenge to biblical authority.

When the charismatic interpreter of the text supplants the authority of the text, a different course is determined. Smith and the Calvary movement would keep the biblical text as the word of God as the epistemological foundation of the textual community and remain subject to its authority. Wimber's comments, "Well,

---

54. Davis, interview.

55. Fromm, "Textual Communities," 275.

56. Fromm, "Textual Communities," 277.

57. Fromm, "Textual Communities," 278.

58. Fromm, "Textual Communities," 276.

the Lord is not limited to His Word . . . The Lord is greater than His Word,"[59] opposes the point that the Bible is the final authority.

Wimber's words are from a secondary source taken from a planning meeting, occurring forty years ago in closed session, without meeting minutes, as recalled by Smith as told to Fromm. This represents the fundamental point of departure of the two waves and is outside the scope of this study. Both Wimber's published works and the trajectory of the two movements lend credence to the veracity of quoted Wimber's statements. When scripture is only one authority among others, it weakens the Bible as the standard of life and godliness (2 Pet 1:3—3:11).

Smith's response at the planning session was to request Wimber's worship team lead the worship and model it for the other senior pastors of the various Calvary Chapels and Vineyards. Smith also suggested that churches that want to emphasize different qualities simply change their name. Wimber instead opts to strike out in a new direction and casts the Vineyard vision.[60]

Striking the balance is a principle to not divide God's people over non-essential issues. However, the authority of the biblical text is itself essential, if it is to regulate matters of faith, practice, and worship. With no text, there is no epistemological foundation for a textual community. Smith purposely allowed the issue to rest with the Lord as to each ministry's fruitfulness and reflects Smith's desire to not divide or create tension for God's people—another expression of love.

7.2.13 Ventures of Faith

Chapter twelve concludes the *Distinctives* and Smith worships, sharing, "It's a thrill to see how God is blessing when we dare to step out and allow Him to do what He wants to do, giving ourselves

59. Fromm, "Textual Communities," 279.
60. Fromm, "Textual Communities," 281.

over as instruments through which He can do what He wants to do if He so desires."[61]

In one sense stepping out in faith is what the worship leader does every time he or she is privileged with the task of leading the congregation in worship as the congregation enters into true worship.

> The original fountain of charisma, the origin of the church itself as well as all of creation is an act of God's speech: "Hear, O Israel," "Come follow Me," "And God said, 'Let there be Light.'" This spoken Word of God is then routinized into a Scriptural text that must always be re-voiced, reinterpreted, transformed from the dead letter on the page into the Word that lives in our hearts by the inspired breath of the proclaimed and divine grace granted to the hearers.[62]

A second essential aspect is to proclaim the word or hear the word proclaimed, "The shared experience of hearing its proclamation is itself constitutive of community."[63] Fromm mentions a third key, which is a combining of the first two, that churches cultivate the gifts of the Spirit in such a way that they grow and replicate.[64] Fromm notes, "If the community is properly constituted around the proclamation of the Word, then those that hear the Word and follow the call will naturally become carriers of the message, and new communities will naturally form as outgrowth and outreaches of the original."[65]

7.3 PARTICIPANT UNIFORMITY

All participants matured and developed spiritually as a result of CCCM's ministry. In effect, CCCM became a farm system for

---

61. Smith, *Calvary Chapel Distinctives*, 115.

62. Fromm, "Textual Communities," 353–54.

63. Fromm, "Textual Communities," 354.

64. Fromm, "Textual Communities," 354.

65. Fromm, "Textual Communities," 354.

these worship leaders to lead worship at CCCM's Sunday morning service and to lead worship in affiliated churches. All the worship leaders agreed on the core values as characteristic of the Calvary Chapel model of ministry. None opposed the distinctive values of the lead pastor who led by example. All saw Smith as the primary worship leader at CCCM, and went on to hold worship leader roles in other affiliated churches.

All reported having a born-again experience and were discipled through CCCM's on-campus ministries. All read their Bibles because it is the word of God and demonstrate a mature biblical worldview. All considered spiritual formation more important than musical ability. Many reported a reconciling of their new identity "in Christ" with their "before Christ" self as musicians. Even if only for hours, these musicians navigated who they were, with who they are now, and with who and what they would become.

Most were multi-instrumentalists, and all sang even if only one claimed voice as their primary instrument. All have published and report that the commercial work was a by-product of their ministry and not a primary goal. Most remained in public ministry at the time of this writing and all their careers have lasted thirty years or longer. All had been in musical outreach projects doing evangelism through music, outside of multiple weekly in-church services. All reported their experiences ministering at CCCM was a significant part of their growth and development as a Christian worshipper.

They see themselves as "sent forth by Holy Ghost" (Acts 13:4)—ministers of music as they actively engaged in a variety of settings such as prayer meetings, home Bible studies, performing with bands in commercial spaces. They served gospel outreaches where praise music was used as an initial draw to gather a group of people to hear the gospel message and to engage in public worship as a witness to not-yet saved people.

These worship leaders' high degree of agreement with Smith's values was extraordinary. The questions allowed them to reflect deeply on their prior experiences at CCCM and by their natural tendency to compare those experiences with their current experiences served to benefit their current practice in leading worship.

The hippies and the traditional conservative evangelicals came to see their conversion experiences as equally valid, an "authenticity that sprang from a personal encounter with Jesus and membership in the faith community."[66] This "once-I-was-lost-but-now-I-am-found" experience becomes a common-to-all story that was scriptural, received, and shared. The common story also provides equal standing before God for everyone in the community.

Smith, as charismatic interpreter of the primary text, showed from the Scriptures to all generations, the bigger picture of what God is doing. The congregation then embodies what Fromm observes as the gospel advancing from generation to generation, "The story of God's Word is the story of the community that forms around the Word . . . nothing less than salvation history itself."[67] CCCM thus reproduces, benefitting from evangelism while preparing for future evangelism.

The differences in preference and style were less important in comparison with the light that shines from an authentic born-again experience transforming the lives of the redeemed at CCCM. Fromm notes the function of style serves the text, not the musical preferences. "Those who knew the tradition of hymn singing from being raised in church were satisfied. Those who did not have the cultural background knew that the hymns are expressive of 'us,' and they did their best to participate and learn."[68]

When considering Jesus' teaching to the woman at the well (John 4:22–24) and in conjunction with the great Commission (Matt 28:18–20), the Lord has charged His church to reproduce more worshippers to the glory of God. Smith's worship service provided the continuity that people needed to fulfill the Great Commission. "It's just God honoring His Word as he said He would."[69]

---

66. Fromm, "Textual Communities," 343.

67. Fromm, "Textual Communities," 339.

68. Fromm, "Textual Communities," 188–89.

69. Laurie, "Chuck Smith Interview."

At CCCM, the worship leader role is best viewed as an extension of the lead pastor role, bringing greater variety to the congregational singing portions of the liturgy. Smith desired to include variety with familiarity over the years. Worship leaders acknowledged that Sunday mornings were very traditional in style despite the public perception of CCCM as being the "hippie church." As Smith's years of service rolled on with overseeing outreach, evangelism, equipping, edifying, and sending out the called, CCCM's liturgical structure remained unchanged and unrivaled.

8

A Human Be-In, In the Spirit

THE RENEWALIST POSITION OF Calvary Chapel Costa Mesa
(CCCM) in the body of Christ is affirmed by two characteristics
of Pentecostals. First is the born-again experience wherein the
Holy Spirit indwells the believer. Second is the empowerment and
overflow of the Holy Spirit's presence and power in one's daily life.
These rest on the authoritative foundation on Jesus Christ the living word of God. Hippies seeking truth from experiences became
disillusioned by the false hope of pop culture, but they found real
love, real peace, and real hope in a relationship with God in Christ.
CCCM's ministry has been paradigmatic, although unique unto
itself.

The four waves of Pentecostal faith of the twentieth century
reveals that CCCM coheres closest with the *Second Wave of Pentecostalism*—also known as the spiritual renewal movement (as discussed in chapter three). Historically, the second wave of renewal
is characterized by normalizing elements of first-wave Pentecostal
worship expressions, grounding individual experiences to Scripture. Smith's challenge beginning in the late 1940s and through the
1950s was to moderate excessive, over-the-top behaviors within a
first-wave Pentecostal denomination. Academia correlates the second wave as adapting Pentecostal elements and integrating them

in non-Pentecostal congregations. Thus, academia has mischaracterized Smith's place in church history.

CCCM was a dominant influence in the Jesus movement and subsequently influenced other lead pastor/worship leader tandem relationships across evangelicalism. Since the Holy Spirit maintains the vibrancy of the textual community, the Bible retains foundational authority for the community's relationship to God and each other.

8.1 BEING THERE

Worship leaders being there in a fruitful ministry context at the same location and with the same liturgy as charismatic interpreters produced data that corresponds and coheres. The degree of coherence is uniform. The continuity over time that resulted from an unchanged liturgy—biblically derived—from December 1965 to October 2013 produced a stable situation that yielded high quality, dense, qualitative data.

The uniformity of responses across the three dimensions of interactions, continuity, and situation leads one to understand that the findings are trustworthy, credible, and reliable. As these worship leaders served in a paradigmatic model of fruitful ministry, there is strong reason to conclude these findings possess a transcendent quality that will transfer across time to guide and inform twenty-first century iterations of this model. Finally, because the Calvary Chapel model has been reiterated thousands of times and persists today, one finds a self-evincing model.

8.1.1 The Lead Pastor is the Primary Worship Leader

Smith never intended that one should work alone in the role of charismatic interpreter of the text in a New Testament church. At a minimum, the non-denominational, independent church leader co-labors with the word of God and the Holy Spirit, as the Spirit of Christ indwells the servant to serve the text to a textual community.

Smith went into ministry with his newly wed bride after WWII, and they identified others to assist in the work of the ministry. He viewed Christian worship as a privilege and a biblical imperative for every born-again believer; thus, he could never abrogate the role. Nonetheless, he shared the leadership role with others to lead the ritual of congregational singing "in psalms, hymns and spiritual songs" (Col 3:16) and to "sing unto the Lord a new song" (Ps 96:1; 98:1; 149:1; Isa 42:10).

Smith created the office of Worship Leader at CCCM in 1985 distinct from the Assistant Pastor and years after the explosive growth of the Jesus movement. The first worship leader at CCCM was another husband-and-wife tandem co-ministering and subordinate to the lead pastor. The lead pastor/worship leader tandem (along with assistant pastors and ushers) represented the visible part of ministry to a worshipping congregation. Smith saw and served the Sunday morning congregation as a mixed multitude—a public gathering of visitors, curious non-believers, seekers, believing visitors, and the regular church family for a public Christian worship service. He biblically designed the service for CCCM to encounter God and be a living witness of the body of Christ engaged in worship.

8.1.2 The Lead Pastor Provides the Vision for Worship

Smith (or an assistant) led congregational singing with piano and organ accompaniment exclusively out of their hymnals from 1965–1985. From 1985–2013, contemporary Christian music supplemented hymn singing since both became a part of the historicity of the Christian church. Smith formed *Maranatha! Music* (M!M) in 1971—not because he loved the style, but because he saw how "Jesus Music" could draw and disciple young people into a maturing relationship with Jesus Christ. He tolerated the style because of its effect on a lost generation.

The earliest albums were often samplers of various artists so Jesus Music bands could sell it to fund outreach ministry. CCCM originated and proliferated "Jesus Music" contemporaneous with the explosive growth of the "Jesus Movement," which sought to worship in the musical vernacular of the day. Smith as primary worship leader of CCCM founded M!M and made key production decisions such as which songs and artists were recorded and distributed. By 1985, the genre was historically authentic to CCCM. Integration with the hymnal provided greater historicization for the movement and variety within their unchanging low-liturgy service.

8.2 TESTIMONIES FROM THE PULPIT AND THE MUSIC STAND

8.2.1 Lived Experiences in Fruitful Ministry

The interviews revealed that the worship leaders each had a John 3:7 born-again experience as a follower of Jesus. Second, they each had an experience in which God had placed a calling on their lives to serve the body of Christ. Third, each experienced empowerment by the Holy Spirit subsequent to their calling as part of their preparation for service. As Smith taught, "It's one thing to have the Holy Spirit poured into your life, and another thing to allow the Holy Spirit to pour out of your life. That's the necessary dynamic for the ministry. Even the disciples were not permitted to engage in the ministry until they had received this dynamic of the Spirit."[1] Musical training varied and occurred independently of empowerment for service.

Fourth, all agree that ministry is a spiritual calling, and each was led in an ongoing walk in the Spirit in his or her personal worship lives. Their continuing walk in the Spirit involved prayer, a hunger for the word of God, a personal worship life, and a vital connection to the body of Christ through serving in a church. As CCCM worshiped publicly, the Holy Spirit led the worship leader individually, who, as a visible agent, led the congregation to give glory to God. The Holy Spirit then subjectively ministered to the worshipping community as He willed. The worship leader

1. Smith, *Calvary Chapel Distinctives*, 31.

continued in the Spirit, engaged in prayer, shared the joy of worship, and relied upon God to faithfully do what the Scripture said He will do.

The lead pastor of a church is the worship leader, and Smith chose to share the role with people endemic to the style of ministry. In so doing, the lead pastor changed from "the worship leader" to "a worship leader." In a sense, the changed lives of the newer worship leaders are evidence of the fruit of the ministry. As a result, each was intimately familiar with the ministry style. Smith shared the worship leader role to extend the influence of the body of Christ's ministry on earth and continued the work of the Lord to disciple and lead others in their calling. He led people who, like him, were subject to Scripture and directed their worship of God and ministerial activities according to the text of Scripture.

The song service promoted the unity that Jesus Christ promotes. The worship leaders created a space for the Holy Spirit to subjectively minister to needs in the congregation as He wills. The worship leader was not to direct the congregation in specified behaviors or to use music or musicianship to elicit an emotional response. Christ held the worship leader's attention—their living example directed the congregation to Christ. Key performance tasks were to support the biblical text, bring the congregation into unity, and to eliminate distractions. The worship leader simply and authentically worshipped God and publicly enjoyed God's presence as they worshipped. Others followed the example of the visible leader as the Spirit of the Lord led them to worship. Scripture regulated the decorum of public meetings, framing the response of the community.

The subjective work of the Spirit was unseen but manifested objectively in the love of God flowing through the congregation and the subsequent evidence of a changed life—the fruit of the fruitful ministry. The Sunday morning worship service was one part of an educative process directed toward equipping the body of Christ to fulfill God's calling in the individual lives of the congregation.

The Sunday morning congregation worshipping together was a mixture of believers and unbelievers. CCCM provided a missional setting for the body of Christ to be a living witness of Jesus Christ on earth. The unity of the Spirit carried through their responsive reading and the Sunday morning teaching, connecting people to the word of God while the Holy Spirit matured believers. The evidence of the Spirit moving is individuals experiencing and demonstrating God's love—not sign gifts, power gifts, or excessive emotional outbursts—producing an obedience of the faith, "which was once delivered unto to the saints" (Jude 1:3).

The worship leaders testified that they sensed something extraordinary—a dynamic in congregational worship—which they attributed to the Holy Spirit working among the worshippers. As the Spirit moved subjectively among the continuum of seekers, non-believers, believing visitors, curious and the regular church family at a Sunday morning service, they described varied responses to the presence of God in worship: tears of joy, conviction of sin leading to repentance, gratitude for salvation, a sense of awe and wonder, and the desire to be still in the presence of God.

They witnessed the family of God that transcended demographic differences such as age, social status, cultural background, and power dynamics. Diversity and inclusivity yielded to the unity of the Spirit. *Agape* is the term among the textual community reserved to capture this unique quality of love and communion that originated within the triune God. As Fischer recounts, "When newcomers came to Calvary, often they would say that the love they experienced was almost palpable."[2]

8.2.2 What is the Lead Pastor/ Worship Leader relationship?

The primary leadership method was that of the leader setting a biblical example, and the ultimate leader was Jesus. Jesus taught his disciples to judge a tree by its fruit (Matt 12:33). The fruit on

---

2. Fischer, *I Remember*, 69.

the tree was present. The charismatic interpreters who shared the role with Smith were also the fruit of the ministry. This became a self-vindication of the ministry methods and demonstrated that God works according to his word and through that context develops confident disciples. This setting produced tremendous unity, but not uniformity, among the worship leaders as they served with their lead pastor. Each retained his or her own personal, distinctive relationship with Christ who prepares His disciples for the ministry of equipping the saints.

Originally, Smith became an independent pastor because he required autonomy to lead as the word of God and the Spirit of the Lord directed him to lead (and not encumbered by a central authority or elder control) with a clear conscience before God. He gave to others the latitude to follow Christ that He desired. He was unwilling to mediate between a Spirit-filled believer and his Savior, preferring to exhort them to seek the Savior themselves.

A non-denominational setting elevated the congregation to pursue a closer walk in the Spirit and beyond the negative stereotypes associated with extremes of Pentecostal faith, which is consistent with second wave spiritual renewalist tendencies. Smith's aim was to present charismatic Christianity as coherently biblical, normal, and a desirable lifestyle. This is novel and overlooked by researchers of Pentecostalism.

A common response of the newer believer to the Holy Spirit's ministry was at first unclear in the mind at the outset but once received and found biblically grounded attracted believers who matured and became fruitful. People wanted to become more pleasing to God according to the Scripture. Smith, according to the *Golden Rule* (Matt 7:12), consequently placed high regard on personal autonomy and highly valued biblically undergirded autonomy among leadership.

Since each leader was accountable to God as Smith was, and since Smith knew the Lord would lead them and develop them according to His plans and purposes, similar to how the Lord had led him, Smith saw his role as one of trusting and testing according to Matthew 13:12. Good stewardship yields greater increase, and concurrent with the increase, more of the master's goods are entrusted to the faithful steward. This is the leadership pattern that Smith endorsed; the steward's value was shown by the steward's faithfulness in managing the household of God. Situations of testing and trusting that required the steward to make choices, revealed the steward's heart.

Smith retained the power to intervene. He, too, was accountable to the Lord as the lead pastor. However, his leadership style showed that he preferred to have the Lord develop leaders by having them seek the Lord in prayer, act according to the word of God, and be discipled by the Lord, much as God had graciously trained him. He encouraged people to prayerfully take steps of faith within the counsel of Scripture. There was no penalty for a good faith effort that failed because Smith understood that stepping out in faith pleased God (Heb 11:6).

Smith knew to abandon an activity no longer producing fruit saying, "Well, I'm not married to it." Smith had no problem replacing something that was not producing fruit. He was willing to give time to let a venture of faith grow. He encouraged people to face adversity to see that venture of faith through to its culmination. Yet, when he sensed it had achieved God's intended purpose or it was no longer fruit-producing, he let it go intending to seek God for another faith venture.

Smith set a high standard of conduct for himself and was self-disciplined to trust God to empower him to meet the challenges of ministry. He did not impose his personal convictions upon others. He trusted that work to the Holy Spirit being active in the life of the believer as the Spirit had personally led him. In other words, Smith trusted the same discipleship process that made him the believer he was, God would use with others. Jesus Christ's work on the cross created a unity of the Spirit amplified by a human unity of purpose to worship in Spirit and in truth. He preferred to set the example of how to be discipled by walking in the Spirit and was reluctant to tell people what to do. If asked, he would direct, but kept a light hand on stylistic preferences so long as he saw the objective fruit of love manifested and the fulfillment of the Great Commission.

Smith was an astute observer when looking for fruit. Each was to stand, independent, on their own before God, but dependent upon and accountable to God (Rom 14:4, 11–12). As lead pastor, he interpreted the human responses from interactions with the Holy Spirit and to give a context—a biblical grounding—that normalized these experiences as biblically comprehensible. Thus, new believers learned how to rely on the Bible for life and godliness as they learned to walk in the Spirit. They learned to appreciate the synergistic effect of the holy Scripture combined with the Holy Spirit to bring authentic, personal spiritual renewal to their life as a born-again believer.

On the other hand, Smith was adamant to honor regulative principles of Scripture. One example was that no flesh should glory in God's presence (Jer 9:24; 1 Cor 1:29–30). In the Sunday morning worship setting, the focus was to keep Christ as the central person of the service for everyone in the service.

Pastor Smith did not allow extreme Pentecostal expressions of spiritual giftings in the Sunday morning service because it went against the New Testament principles of decorum for a public meeting, as detailed in 1 Corinthians 12–14. Also, the ordinance of communion was reserved for the family of God that met on the third Thursday of each month due to a Scriptural precedent set forth in 1 Corinthians 11:27–29. Not serving communion to the faithful in a public setting was an act of consideration for the welfare of the unbeliever's soul and for the timing of service. The Sunday morning worship service was a public meeting that invited a mixed multitude.

Servant leadership set the tone. Smith was not a micromanager. His example was caught and secondarily taught only if necessary. Smith taught that all are subject to the text and Holy Spirit led. If exposed to a consistent biblical example, one would know what to do and how to act. Specific instruction came through conveying an understanding of scripture and how applying biblical principles led to proper conduct.

There was no room for Smith on the epistemic point of any charismatic interpreter setting himself as authoritatively equivalent to Scripture. In contradiction to this principle was John Wimber, who began taking on "An authority that is self-referential and self-determining. Wimber was now standing in the authority of the Prophet."[3] Smith's adherence to the text as the primary objective authority to guide faith and practice that regulates life in the subjective experience of the Holy Spirit led to Wimber's founding of the Vineyard movement and separating from Calvary Chapel affiliation. Vineyard began the self-proclaimed denomination of the *Third Wave of Pentecostalism*.[4]

The relational dynamics between the lead pastor and worship leader were bound by ministry. The lead pastor and worship leader saw themselves as servants of God. Smith believed titles could potentially inflame pride and his experience showed that titles often become an obstacle to fruitful ministry. The understanding was that each one's service was equally valid before God, and each was to defer to the other in their specified role to accomplish the ministry tasks that God set before His servants. More specifically, each was appointed by God as stewards of God's house with specific domains that could fluctuate over time. Smith also believed that as one walks in the Spirit, everything serves as preparation for something else, culminating in heavenly rewards due to faithful service. Ministry, independent of salvation, flowed out as an expression of love and gratitude returned to God for all He has done.

There was no mention among the worship leaders of personal interaction of relationship outside of ministry. Smith appeared singularly focused on ministry and learned how the Holy Spirit revitalized him as he ministered. He took vacations, but they were truly just more opportunities to minister in other settings. During the summers, Smith would go to camp as a camp counselor, overseer, and minister to youth. When he traveled to Hawaii on vacation, it was to speak at affiliated churches and perhaps devote

3. Fromm, "Textual Communities," 276.
4. Fromm, "Textual Communities," 282.

some time for thanksgiving and praising God for His glorious creation while surfing.

Life in Christ as a living sacrifice is full of ministry opportunities, and everything prepared the servant of God for something else. The Holy Spirit revives his servant as the servant serves by walking in the power of the Spirit and not in the power of the flesh. This was Smith's safeguard against pastoral burnout. Smith had dedicated his life to serving the Lord, and he was very good at serving God. No worship leader mentioned a social occasion with Smith that did not involve some aspect of ministry. Small talk was rare and revolved around health and family. The worship leaders related to Smith through ministering.

Biblically, the lead pastor/worship leader relationship advanced by the pattern set by the parable of the talents (Matt 25:14–30). Christ, as Lord and master, appoints stewards. Each steward is given a portion of the master's goods according to his ability. Each steward makes the most of what his master had entrusted to him, and he is accountable to their master for his stewardship of his master's property. Upon the master's return, accounts are settled, and each is rewarded in proportion to his faithful service.

Applying the parable in this setting, the master who went on a long journey is Jesus. The master's goods are the gifts given to each steward. The steward is the minister, and the increase in gifts goes to the benefit of the master's estate.

In ministry at CCCM, each was responsible for conducting their appointed tasks. Each was given the liberty to address their tasks biblically but with wide latitude. With the biblical lens, Smith stated that the church is Christ's church (Matt 16:18). Jesus is the head of the church who builds his church. This relieved the pressures surrounding trying to do the work of God with human strength. There would be no taking on tasks and responsibilities that were only God's to do. Nevertheless, it was understood that Jesus appointed stewards to tend to the household of God and Jesus would settle accounts with His servants. This understanding frames the relational dynamics between worship leader and lead pastor.

8.2.3 Why Were There No Worship Wars?

The answer stems first from the biblical text itself and then its charismatic interpreter. First, there are multiple textual commands. For example, there is a command from the Old Testament—"Sing unto the LORD a new song, and his praise from the end of the earth" (Isa 42:10). Similarly, there are New Testament commands as with Paul's admonition to the Colossians—"Let the word of Christ dwell in you richly in all wisdom; teaching and admonishing one another in psalms and hymns and spiritual songs, singing with grace in your hearts to the Lord" (Col 3:16). Everyone is subject to the text in a textual community, which specifies new songs and a variety of songs. So, as the community sought an authoritative link to authentic Christianity, they yielded personal preference (subjective) to the Scripture (objective).

Second, the charismatic interpreter biblically confronted issues of style. This subjective point of difference exemplifies how the community objectively showed that "The fruit of the Spirit is love" (Gal 5:22). The young people favored rock-styled music and many of them, being unchurched, had no connection with hymns. They were taught to realize that the hymns placed them in a line of Christian faith that descended from a practice in which Jesus had participated. "And when they had sung a hymn, they went out into the mount of Olives" (Matt 26:30).

They realized their new relationship in Christ would embody things that Jesus did. This was one small, authentic way they could become more Christ-like. This was especially easy because of the reciprocal response from the existing congregation who welcomed them and their music.

Those favoring hymns understood that accepting new believers' music meant accepting the new believer. It was a God-given opportunity for elder believers to enjoy the revitalizing benefit of fellowshipping with new believers and seeing the Lord moving in the lives of young people. The realization that everybody needs Jesus, that everybody needs the forgiveness that only Jesus provides, and that the born-again experience makes them the family of God.

The established believers were a part of a dynamic church that was growing and fulfilling the great commission.

Additionally, they could see that the worship the new believers offered, expressed in a new song, was God-honoring, even if the style was unconventional. The new believers demonstrated authentic praise and worship as equally valid and vibrant to that of their own, even if the styles of dress and comportment did not match. Everyone was prized and appreciated—the zeal of the new believer and the faith walk of the mature believer—each side benefited the other as complementary rather than in opposition.

Another new revelation was the motivational and emotional importance of the belief in the imminent return of Christ. There is a unique contribution that belief in the pretribulation return of Christ has upon the urgency and focus to go according to the Great Commission and the mission of the church.

Finally, there is a greater understanding of the epistemic issue that divides the *Second Wave of Pentecostalism* from the third and fourth waves of Pentecostalism. Beliefs germane to the Christian faith are grounded in Scripture. Therefore, the Scripture itself cannot be replaced regarding its primary place of authority. Jesus, as the cornerstone, laying the foundation for the Church (Eph 2:20) also promises emotional comfort, "I will not leave you comfortless" (John 14:18). When those truths are combined with the apostle's command to "Comfort one another with these words" (1 Thess 4:18), it is evident that when the Scripture is consistently interpreted and authentically lived, Jesus has provided all we need for "life and godliness" (2 Pet 1:3).

8.3 THE LOW LITURGY IS HIGHLY ESTEEMED

Even after a contemporary worship leader was brought on and, eventually, a worship team developed, they were only utilized on alternating Sundays. Every Sunday morning service opened with a congregational hymn, singing from the hymnal, which was led by piano and organ. Psalm 100:4 says, "Enter into his gates with thanksgiving, and into his courts with praise: be thankful unto him and bless his name." This command was literally taken and faithfully implemented with organ and piano accompaniment for congregational singing. Special songs were rare. Smith or an assistant pastor typically led the congregation singing.

There could be up to three songs with all verses sung. All songs selected to supplement the teaching. A traditional offertory—usually featuring organ and piano as an instrumental offering—was presented while receiving the offering as an act of worship. It was here where a guest vocalist would rarely sing a special song. The offertory also functioned on alternating weeks to permit the worship team to be ready to lead the second song service. Weeks that did not have contemporary music simply continued a second segment of congregational singing, up to three songs out of the hymnal, which led to the responsive Scripture reading and then the morning message.

In 1985, the second segment of the congregation worshipping in song would alternate weeks between hymn singing or the contemporary Christian music choruses supplemented with updated hymns and arranged for the worship team. This pattern of ministry is out of step and far behind most other affiliated churches that abandoned or never used hymn singing when they began. The Sunday morning service at CCCM was traditional, but often alternated to blended service. The contemporary services with all the hippies performing occurred at evening services since the youth movement began. The worship leaders all said the order of the service never changed.

What did change was the variety within some sections and the time allotted for each section. With Smith's arrival, the pace of the service noticeably ticked upward. The efficiency of the use of time was a hallmark of Smith's stewardship. Smith started precisely on time, in keeping with the decorum of a publicly announced meeting, and every minute was purposeful. This showed care and thoughtfulness for people who may be visitors or for those who were curious.

8.4 PRACTICAL APPLICATIONS
IN THE WORSHIP SERVICE

The textual community is the entire congregation, including leadership (who may be more accountable). All are subject to the text, as seen in the opening to the Philippians: "Paul and Timotheus, the servants of Jesus Christ, to all the saints in Christ Jesus which are at Philippi, with the bishops and deacons" (Phil 1:1). All are autonomous and willingly become subject to the text—no one has greater authority than the text. Believers are obligated and privileged by God's grace to study through the entire text to discover His revelation of Himself.

Charismatic interpreters re-spirit the inspired text for a listening audience. Since they serve a literate audience, they attend a Bible reading program. With *lectio continua*—exposition by chapter and verse teaching—the charismatic interpreter leads the congregation through the text employing a consistent literal interpretation across genres. They do not imagine or re-imagine a new meaning but seek to reveal the implications that God provides through the human agent that God inspired to write the text.

Since God's word is inexhaustible (Rom 11:33), the intent is to re-spirit the text so as to serve each successive generation. In this sense, no revolution is needed or intended. It is the everlasting God revealing himself through willing human agents across time. Jesus—as the ultimate revelation of God for humanity—is building his church. There is no need to re-imagine the text in novel ways.

The charismatic interpreter grows the textual community in maturity by understanding the inexhaustible text to see new implications and applications from the text for their generation. God means what He says, which is interpreted by human authors. God is there, and he does speak. The meaning of the biblical text is singular, but with an unfathomable depth of application. When a community takes God seriously and learns how to live lives pleasing to Him through a maturation process of abiding, that community houses the spiritual gifts that Jesus Christ bestows on each generation until His return.

A Human Be-In, In the Spirit

The charismatic interpreter is born-again, called, empowered, and lives in the Spirit, believing in the finished work of Christ according to the word of God. Having received multiple gifts beginning with a new birth, charismatic interpreters are subsequently graced with an ability to re-spirit the text to serve a listening community. Re-spiriting the text represents the text as the pure word of God by the Holy Spirit who inspired the text.

On the other hand, reimagining the text risks leading people by a product of the human mind and away from the mind of God. Mary, the mother of Jesus, said, "He hath shewed strength with his arm; he hath scattered the proud in the imagination of their hearts" (Luke 1:51). Imagining and re-imagining the ways of God when God has already revealed them, aggrandizes human thinking and invites error.

Humans, capable of taking the word of God seriously, fully engage the text aided by the same Spirit who inspired the text is a clearer path to accurately represent the text to each succeeding generation rather than to imagine or re-imagine what God has said. Re-imagining the text for others risks becoming self-referential. The self-referential leader ascends from a servant-leader position into a peer position with God as God's representative. This is contrary to John 3:30, which says, "He must increase, but I must decrease."

Each generation is tasked to interpret what God originally meant in the original context for the benefit of the congregation they serve. This study shows that by teaching, playing music, and simply reading the word of God aloud, a generation came to the salvation that Jesus provides and matured in that faith with the ability to reproduce in kind.

Smith continually reminded M!M artists and leaders of the necessity of total reliance on God to do the work of God in God's way. God's people have gifts, skills, and abilities, but apart from God, they can do nothing. Jesus stated boldly, "I am the vine, ye are the branches: He that abideth in me, and I in him, the same bringeth forth much fruit: for without me ye can do nothing" (John 15:5).

8.5 EVERY WORD MATTERS

The rituals of the community are communication-based. All the worship leaders expressed this theme. Their stewardship of the text extended into the lyrical content that it served an intentional purpose. Biblically-based purposes exist to support the teaching of the biblical text, give meaningful verbal expression for new believers to worship in Spirit and in truth with understanding, and unify the congregation to praise God. CCCM-praising *ensemble* served the Holy Spirit with a visible witness so that the Spirit of Christ could attract, convict, and otherwise minister to all individuals visiting the body of Christ assembled in Costa Mesa.

Special performance-based music where the congregation becomes passive spectators may serve a limited purpose in a service, but the biblical directive is for everyone to sing unto the Lord a new song and to admonish one another in songs and hymns and spiritual songs making melody in their hearts. The Holy Spirit intentionally left these scriptural commands open-ended so that God and humans can enjoy variety. Therefore, there is a latitude in the way songs are implemented—the instrumentation, the presentation, the style of music—to avoid the staleness of a forced ritual.

The Holy Spirit provides variety so servants may lead others away from the danger that Jesus referred to: "Well hath Esaias prophesied of you hypocrites, as it is written, This people honoureth me with their lips, but their heart is far from me" (Mark 7:6). With variety and by the continual filling and refilling of the Holy Spirit the textual community is to "be filled with the Spirit. Speaking to yourselves in psalms and hymns and spiritual songs, singing and making melody in your heart to the Lord; Giving thanks always for all things unto God and the Father in the name of our Lord Jesus Christ; Submitting yourselves one to another in the fear of God" (Eph 5:18[b]–21).

The ultimate source for legitimization through historicization is the biblical text itself and not any tradition, practice, or emotion. The book of Acts was seen as both descriptive, historical narrative and prescriptive for implementation today. The foundational cornerstone is Jesus Christ—laid in the first century and declared for the church in Ephesians 2:11–22. All the rest are living stones on the foundation for God's glory. Scriptural examples follow principles but need not remain primitive. The Holy Spirit wants to work and move among the church in each generation according to his word and by the indwelling Spirit of Christ (Rom 8:9).

8.6 LIVING ACTS 29

The book of Acts has 28 chapters, and it has been said the faithful are writing the twenty-ninth chapter day-by-day. One might ask, where are these five worship leaders now? Was their individual fruitfulness inextricably tied to their relationship with Smith? This would have been antithetical to the ministry of Smith who trusted believers in Christ to the word of God and the Spirit of God to produce the fruit of fruitful ministry. As of this writing, each is still serving as the Lord has continued to lead him or her. All continue in biblical marriage. The faithfulness of these worship leaders with the *charisms* the Lord has given them has multiplied and as in the Parable of the Talents (Matt 25:14–30), more has been given to them. They all continue in fruitful ministry.

8.7 CONCLUSION

Thus, Pastor Chuck Smith's trajectory is nothing less than heaven-bound. His faith in the word of God, so certain and his personal habits so disciplined, he remained committed to walk the congregation of CCCM through the Bible each Sunday before his passing in 2013. Chuck Smith truly lived "As If" Jesus could return at any moment. He was ready to meet Jesus in the air with the faithful as the apostle Paul mentions, "And to wait for his Son from heaven, whom he raised from the dead, even Jesus, which delivered us from the wrath to come" (1 Thess 1:10). The Rapture of the church was not just a doctrine of mental assent for him—it was the foundation for daily living in hope and expectancy. He would station himself at his post, ever watching, and awaiting the Lord's imminent return.

As for Smith's ministry to the hippie generation, contrary to some recent exposés, the Jesus movement was not a revolution. A revolution does not normally persist across generations, although oppressors and tyrants may remain after a revolution. These people—the hippies—were looking for a new way of life, a new community, and a new leader. Smith, not being a cult leader, actively pointed them to Christ and not himself. Jesus' intention is for the church to be led by Himself (Col 1:18).

Charismatic interpreters steward the gifts of God in the church age. The prophetic fulfillment of Joel 2:28–29, recognized by the Apostle Peter in Acts 2 and delineated by the Apostles in the New Testament as the extension of the Old Testament (Heb 9:15), pointed to the coming Savior of the world, who pours out his Spirit in these last days (Acts 2:17). As Moses was a faithful steward, Jesus (the more faithful steward over a greater stewardship) has assigned a stewardship to each believer. A charismatic interpreter is one form of that stewardship.

By the sense of sight, the first-century Christian church differs from the twenty-first century church, but the Spirit that poured out then is identical. Acts 2:37–47 remains applicable as the Holy Spirit continues to pour out upon faithful followers to charismatically interpret God's Word to listening, receptive hearers. Each successive generation continues to receive the outpouring and responds in worship until "the promise of the Father" (Luke 24:49; Acts 1:4), which is the promise of the Holy Spirit (Acts 2:33), is fully realized.

Fruitful ministry is a lifetime of commitment through paths of hardship and joy with the Spirit of Christ (Rom 8:9) leading to eternal rewards. One should expect the continuance of repentance and baptism in Jesus' name for the remission of sins and the indwelling of the Holy Spirit as a valid promise from the word of God. Luke described that which persists today, "And they, continuing daily with one accord in the temple, and breaking bread from house to house, did eat their meat with gladness and singleness of heart, praising God and having favor with all people. And the Lord added to the church daily such as should be saved" (Acts 2:46–47).

As the Lord our God calls each successive generation until his return, the Holy Spirit will continue to graciously pour out, leading to salvation through faith in Jesus Christ. Worship in fruitful ministry, unbroken communion with God—personal and congregational—continues.

Afterword

HAVING LIVED THE JESUS movement in my youth and seeing the rapid rise of Calvary Chapels throughout the United States (and around the world), I find it interesting that Calvary Chapel does not fit in any of the supposed four waves. In fact, Calvary Chapel (and other pop-up denominations of the day) were affiliated with something that had broader impact—the Jesus movement. The reason why I believe Calvary Chapel does not fit into any of the four waves is because charismatic renewal predominantly affected a narrow group of churches.

Whereas the Jesus movement did not just affect a narrow group of churches, it influenced an entire culture, and due to its massive impact, it changed the way a generation of believers worshipped God. While it is true that the initial move of God was predominantly amongst the hippies, who were disenfranchised youth, it quickly spread across generations and denominations with an apocalyptic message of salvation—Jesus is coming soon, are you ready to meet Him?

Pastor Chuck's teaching on the imminent return of Jesus and Lonnie Frisbee's preaching on the nearness of God worked hand-in-hand quickly resulting in massive growth through people of all ages professing faith in Jesus. This massive response to the Gospel resulted in an outpouring of new songs and new methods of evangelism as street preachers and bands teamed up and proclaimed Jesus at high schools, in parks, and street corners all around the world. In Pastor Chuck's assessment, this new movement of the Spirit had less in common with the waves of charismatic renewal and more in common with the original Jesus movement of the book of Acts. Thus, the move of the Spirit that gave birth to Calvary Chapel could not be identified with the narrow group of charismatic churches; it was something much greater. It was a true revival.

One of the characteristics of a true revival is the tangible experience of the real presence of God. That is one of the characteristics of the worship experience that I had in Calvary Chapel. The greatest sign of the real presence of God is the felt love of God. That was the predominant testimony of those who attended Calvary Chapel during the height of revival. There was an overwhelming sense of God's love and acceptance.

Pastor David Rosales of Calvary Chapel, Chino Valley told me of the first time he went to Calvary Chapel. He was drunk and stoned and knew he would be escorted out. However, much to his surprise, he felt nothing but love and acceptance, which kept him coming back and eventually led to him becoming born again.

The experience of God's love became the foundation for an innocent, childlike faith where people prayed and believed God would answer them. They saw miracle after miracle as God answered prayers for healing, deliverance, provision, even providing a new refrigerator. All of this faith and love fueled the passionate sounds of worship that filled Calvary Chapel.

In the early days, worship was sung acapella, without music. As bands came to Christ, they would write songs about their newfound faith and play them at the various Bible studies. Some of those songs became the songs of praise, especially the songs written directly from Scripture. We loved singing God's word. It was organic and unplanned. There was an innocence in the music.

I think it is important to grasp a sense of the innocence of the times to understand the profound move of the Spirit that resulted in Calvary Chapel Ministries. I was sixteen when I became the worship leader and youth pastor for Calvary Chapel, Vista. That is the first time I heard the term, "worship leader." Before that, we were simply called, "musicians and singers."

When I led worship, you could sense the electricity in the room. I now know that it was the presence of God. We did not know we were in a revival; it was normal church to us. I think that is the difference between all the waves of the charismatic renewal and the Jesus movement. We believed God's word was the blueprint for life and Acts was the model for church life, and we did it.

This simple approach to church spilled over into our practice of worship. We believed that when we worshipped, God was present because his word said so. We did not pray, "Come, Holy Spirit." We knew that he was already with us because his word informed us. From the understanding that God was in our midst, our worship became conversational.

Jesus-people told God how much they loved Him and how thankful they were for all He had done. We did not want the attention on anyone but God in our midst. When someone stood up and started to worship in a more ecstatic way, it took the attention off God and put it on them. It was an interruption to what the Spirit was doing with the rest of us, and we did not like it. We got that value from 1 Corinthians 14. We wanted to focus our attention on Jesus. It was the Word and the Spirit working in unison.

From a theological perspective, I think of the worship that Adam and Eve experienced in the Garden of Eden. They had no separation from God. They had no consciousness of self—no consciousness of sin or guilt. They were only conscious of God himself. However, when sin entered the world, the first reaction was self-consciousness. Adam and Eve hid from God. That has been the problem of worship ever since. Everything that we teach about worship is after the Fall. It is worship in a fallen world. It is worship from a position of being separated from God. Because I feel separated from God, I must draw near. Adam and Eve did not have to draw near to God. They were in a constant awareness of his Presence and the Rabbis tell us they were clothed in his glory.

Of course, every worship team calls attention to itself. A better way is to be so talented that bad playing does not distract anyone from their experience of worship; yet, the tension of self is still there. However, during times of revival, we come back to the simplicity of being in God's Presence and losing all awareness of self and only being consumed with Jesus. In those moments, I still feel the electricity in the room that I felt as I led worship in my early days as a worship leader. That is the closest worship comes to the worship Adam and Eve experienced in the Garden.

One of the stories I will never forget. I played the song, "Heart of Worship," when I led worship at Calvary Chapel Costa Mesa. Pastor Chuck called me into his office and asked me about the song. He said, I have never left the heart of worship. When you sing that song, you are making me say something that is not true. You are manipulating me to have an experience that I have never had. Please do not manipulate me in that way again.

In that moment, I realized I was in the presence of someone who never left the place of revival. He was and continued to be in the flow of the Jesus movement until the day he stepped into eternity with Jesus. That has been the constant desire of my heart—to remain in the flow of the Jesus movement that began in the book of Acts and continued through Calvary Chapel during the Jesus movement. It was the sound of a new generation coming to faith. It was the sound of a new song emerging from newly redeemed hearts. It was the sound of God's word being proclaimed from untrained, uneducated men who have simply been with Jesus. That is the sound of revival and my prayer is, "Let It Rise!"

PASTOR HOLLAND DAVIS (the real PHD)
Founding Pastor and Worship Leader of Calvary Chapel, San Clemente
Award Winning Songwriter of the Maranatha! Music Classic, "Let It Rise"
Author of *Let It Rise: A Manual for Worship*[1]

1. Davis, *Let It Rise.*

Bibliography

Aniol, Scott. *By the Waters of Babylon: Worship in a Post-Christian Culture.* Grand Rapids: Kregel, 2015.

Artman, Amy Collier, and Kate Bowler. *The Miracle Lady: Kathryn Kuhlman and the Transformation of Charismatic Christianity.* Grand Rapids: William B. Eerdmans, 2019.

Balmer, Randall. *Mine Eyes Have Seen the Glory: A Journey into the Evangelical Subculture in America.* 25th Anniversary Edition. New York: Oxford University Press, 2014.

Barna, George. *American Worldview Inventory 2020–21: The Annual Report on the State of Worldview in the United States.* Glendale: Arizona Christian University Press, 2021.

Barna Group, The. "Is American Christianity Turning Charismatic?" January 7, 2008. Barna Group. https://www.barna.com/research/is-american-christianity-turning-charismatic.

Barrett, David. "The Worldwide Holy Spirit Renewal." In *The Century of the Holy Spirit: 100 Years of Pentecostal and Charismatic Renewal,* Nashville: Thomas Nelson, 2001.

Bartoş, Emil. "The Three Waves of Spiritual Renewal of the Pentecostal-Charismatic Movement." *Review of Ecumenical Studies Sibiu* 7.1 (2015) 20–42. DOI: https://doi.org/10.1515/ress-2015-0003.

Beeler, Christmas. "A Generation Led to Jesus." *Calvary Chapel Magazine* 96 (2023) 7.

Billboard Magazine. "Top Records of 1966: Top Singles." *Billboard,* December 24, 1966.

———. "Billboard Hot 100." *Billboard,* July 22, 1967.

Calvary Chapel Association. "Calvary Chapel Association: *Reviving the Systematic Exposition of Scripture*" (2022). https://calvarycca.org.

Calvary Chapel Global Network. "History." Calvary Chapel Global Network. 2022. https://calvarychapel.com/history/.

Christerson, Brad, and Richard Flory. *The Rise of Network Christianity: How Independent Leaders are Changing the Religious Landscape.* New York: Oxford University Press, 2017.

Bibliography

Cowan, Nelson. "Lay-Prophet-Priest: The Not-So-Fledgling "Office" of the Worship Leader." *Liturgy* 32.1 (2017) 24–31. DOI: 10.1080/0458063X.2016.1229443.

Davis, Holland. *Let It Rise: A Manual for Worship*. Alachua: Bridge-Logos, 2009.

DeSelm, Dave. "5 Relational Keys for Senior Pastors and Worship Leaders" 2019. Dave Deselm Ministries, Inc., September 24, 2019. https://www.davedeselmministries.org/blog/5-relational-keys-for-pastors-worship-leaders.

Dueck, Jonathan. *Congregational Music, Conflict and Community* (1st ed.). London: Routledge, 2017. DOI: https://doi-org.ezproxy.liberty.edu/10.4324/9781315546247.

Dylan, Bob. "A Hard Rain's A Gonna Fall." Recorded December 6, 1962. On, *The Free Wheelin' Bob Dylan*, released May 27, 1963, Columbia Records. Official Audio, https://www.youtube.com/watch?v=T5aloHmR4to.

Eckhardt, John. *Moving in the Apostolic: How to Bring the Kingdom of Heaven to Earth*. Grand Rapids: Chosen Books, 2017.

Efron, Sonni. "Calvary Chapel Stands Tall on Fundamentalist Tenets: Religion: Santa Ana Church Draws 12,000 People on Sundays and Operates a Vast Outreach Program." *Los Angeles Times* (October 12, 1990). https://www.latimes.com/archives/la-xpm-1990-10-12-mn-2328-story.html.

English de Alminana, Margaret and Lois E. Olena. *Women in Pentecostal and Charismatic Ministry: Informing a Dialogue on Gender, Church, and Ministry*. Boston: Brill, 2016.

Espinosa, Gastón. *William J. Seymour and the Origins of Global Pentecostalism: A Biography and Documentary History*. Durham: Duke University Press, 2014.

Farlow, Alfred. "The Brotherhood of Man." *The Christian Science Journal* (1893). https://journal.christianscience.com/issues/1893/12/11-9/the-brotherhood-of-man.

Félix-Jäeger, Steven. *Renewal Worship: A Theology of Pentecostal Doxology*. Downers Grove: InterVarsity, 2022.

Fischer, Sharon Gardner. *I Remember . . . The Birth of Calvary Chapel*. Yorba Linda: Sharon Gardner Fischer, 2014.

Foursquare People. "Dick Mills Shares How Foursquare's Founder Impacted His Life." https://resources.foursquare.org/dick_mills_shares_how_foursquares_founder_impacted_his_life.

Fromm, Charles E. "Textual Communities and New Song in the Multimedia Age: The Routinization of Charisma in the Jesus Movement." PhD diss., Fuller Theological Seminary, School of Intercultural Studies, 2006.

Fromm, Chuck. "The Critical Relationship Between Pastor and Worship Leader." *Worship Leader Magazine* (March 4, 2020). https://www.sermoncentral.com/pastors-preaching-articles/chuck-fromm-the-critical-relationship-between-pastor-and-worship-leader-727.

Gainey, Henry. *The Afterglow: Connecting People with their Spiritual Gifts*. Costa Mesa: The Word For Today, 2007.

Bibliography

Garrett, Gary W. "Personal Testimony of Being the First Person to Receive the Holy Ghost at 'Stones Folly' in Topeka, Kansas" (January 1, 1901). Originally published in, *Apostolic Faith April –1951*. Apostolic Archives International Inc. Research Center. https://www.apostolicarchives.com/articles/article/8801925/173171.htm.

Geisler, Norman L. *Systematic Theology [In One Volume]*. Minneapolis: Bethany House, 2011.

———. *Twelve Points that Show Christianity is True: A Handbook on Defending the Christian Faith*. Norm Geisler International Ministries, www.ngim.org, 2016.

Geivett, Douglas R. and Holly Pivec. *A New Apostolic Reformation?: A Biblical Response to a Worldwide Movement*. Ashland: Lexham, 2018.

Gijbers, Victor. "Chapter 4.1: The Hermeneutic Circle." Leiden University Faculty of Humanities. Uploaded September 27, 2017. YouTube video, 12:04. https://www.youtube.com/watch?v=zIEzc__BBxs.

Ginsberg, Allen. *Howl and Other Poems*. San Francisco: City Lights Pocket Bookshop, 1956.

Greear, J. D. "What Every Pastor Wishes His Worship Leader Knew." J. D. Greear Ministries. August 7, 2017. https://jdgreear.com/what-every-pastor-wishes-his-worship-leader-knew.

Grudem, Wayne A. *Systematic Theology: An Introduction to Biblical Doctrine*. Grand Rapids: Zondervan. (2000).

Guzik, David. "Remembering Chuck Smith." Enduring Word (October 3, 2018). YouTube video, 49:07. https://www.youtube.com/watch?v=YnxqJEjKzko.

Hawkes, Paul. "A Critical Analysis of the Third and Fourth Wave of Pentecostalism" DTh. Thesis, University of South Africa, Pretoria, 2009. URL: http://hdl.handle.net/10500/1857.

Hicks, Zac. *The Worship Pastor: A Call to Ministry for Worship Leaders and Teams*. Grand Rapids: Zondervan, 2016.

Higgins, Thomas W. "Kenn Gulliksen, John Wimber, and the Founding of the Vineyard Movement." *Pneuma: The journal of the Society for Pentecostal Studies*. 34.2 (2012) 208–228.

Hilliker, Jim. "*KFSG LA 4Square Gospel: Pioneer L. A. Christian Station Stops Broadcasting After 79 Years*." Radio Heritage Foundation. *http://www.radioheritage.net/Story49.asp*.

Hindson, Edward E. *Glory in the Church: The Coming Revival*. Nashville: Thomas Nelson, 1975.

His Church. "About: Our History" (2022). https://web.archive.org/web/20220814100418/https://hischurch.life/about/.

His Church Calvary Tri City. https://www.facebook.com/CalvaryChapelTriCity/about_details.

History.com Editors. "The Monterey Pop Festival Reaches its Climax." https://www.history.com/this-day-in-history/the-monterey-pop-festival-reaches-its-climax.

Bibliography

Holmes, Arthur F. "A History of Philosophy: 01 The Beginning of Greek History" Wheaton College, Uploaded April 2, 2015, YouTube video, 49:17. https://www.youtube.com/watch?v=YatoZKduW18.

Howard, John Robert. "The Flowering of the Hippie Movement." *Annals of the American Academy of Political and Social Science* 382 (1969) 43–55. https://www.jstor.org/stable/1037113?seq=8.

Hutchinson, Mark. "The Problem with 'Waves': Mapping Charismatic Potential in Italian Protestantism, 1890–1929." *Pneuma: The Journal of the Society for Pentecostal Studies* 39.1–2 (2017) 34–54.

Hycner, Richard H. "Some Guidelines for the Phenomenological Analysis of Interview Data." *Human Studies* 8.3 (1985) 279–303.

Jensen, Lori Jolene. "(Re)Discovering Fundamentalism in the Cultural Margins: Calvary Chapel Congregations as Sites of Cultural Resistance and Religious Transformation." PhD diss., University of Southern California, 2000.

Jeremiah, David. "What Is the Fruit of the Spirit and How Do I Grow It?" *Turning Point for God.* https://davidjeremiah.blog/what-it-really-means-to-bear-fruit-and-how-to-produce-it-in-your-life.

Kaufflin, Bob. *Worship Matters: Leading Others to Encounter the Greatness of God.* Wheaton: Crossway, 2008.

Kilian, Aaron. "The Relationship of a Senior Pastor and Worship Leader: Why It Matters." Shepherds Theological Seminary (May 10, 2022). https://shepherds.edu/the-relationship-of-a-senior-pastor-and-worship-leader-why-it-matters/.

Knox, John. *Sociology is Rude!: A Conversation on Sociological Theory and Thought.* Dubuque: Kendall-Hunt, 2019.

———. "The Spiritual Side of Life." Sacroegoism.com (2023). http://www.sacroegoism.com/blog/2023/9/24/the-spiritual-side-of-life.

Kopp, Bill. "Free Love & LSD: How the 'Human Be-in Launched the Summer of Love." *The San Francisco Standard* (December 24, 2022). https://sfstandard.com/arts-culture/free-love-lsd-how-the-human-be-in-launched-the-summer-of-love.

Laurie, Greg. "Chuck Smith Interview: Icons of Faith Series with Greg Laurie" (October 3, 2013). YouTube video, https://www.youtube.com/watch?v=a64YADx_Ymk.

Laurie, Greg, and Ellen Vaughn. *Jesus Revolution: How God Transformed an Unlikely Generation and How He Can Do It Again Today.* Grand Rapids: Baker Books, 2018.

Leedy, Paul D., et al. *Practical Research: Planning and Design 12th ed.* New York: Pearson, 2019.

Legge, Gordon. "Fourth Wave Under Study: [Final Edition.]" *Calgary Herald* (March 16, 1991): A14.

McKenzie, Scott. Vocalist "San Francisco (Be Sure to Wear Flowers in Your Hair). Produced by Lou Adler and John Phillips. Written by John Philips. Released May 13, 1967.

Bibliography

MacDonald, G. Jeffrey. "Chuck Smith, 86, Dies After Cancer Battle." *Christianity Today* (October 3, 2013). https://www.christianitytoday.com/news/2013/october/chuck-smith-86-dies-after-cancer-battle.html.

MacIntosh, Michael, and Raul Reis. *A Venture of Faith: The History and Philosophy of the Calvary Chapel Movement*. A Michael MacIntosh / Raul Ries Limited Production. Logos Media Group, 1992. Somebody Loves You Media Group (2007). 122 minutes. https://vimeo.com/38234025.

Metaxas, Eric. *Letter to the American Church*. Washington, DC: Salem, 2022.

Meyer, Stephen C. *Return of the God Hypothesis: Three Scientific Discoveries that Reveal the Mind Behind the Universe*. New York: HarperOne, 2021.

Meza, Priscilla. "Phone Interview by author with the Registrar's office of Life Pacific College" (July 16, 2021).

Miller, Donald E. *Reinventing American Protestantism: Christianity in the New Millennium*. Berkeley: University of California Press, 1997.

Miller, Donald E., et al. *Spirit and Power: The Growth and Global Impact of Pentecostalism*. New York: Oxford University Press, 2013. DOI: doi:10.1093/acprof:oso/9780199920570.001.0001.

Miller, Stephen. *Worship Leaders: We Are Not Rock Stars*. Chicago: Moody, 2013.

Morrison, Craig. "The Mamas and the Papas." *Encyclopedia Britannica* (October 17, 2023). https://www.britannica.com/topic/The-Mamas-and-the-Papas.

Nel, Marius. "Rather Spirit-Filled than Learned! Pentecostalism's Tradition of Anti-Intellectualism and Pentecostal Theological Scholarship." *Verbum Et Ecclesia* 37.1 (2016) 1–9.

Niequist, Aaron. "Too Much Bono in the Church?" *Liturgy* 32.1 (2017) 42–45. DOI: 10.1080/0458063X.2016.1229452.

Pappalardo, Chris and Mike Passaro. "What Every Worship Leader Wishes the Pastor Knew." J. D. Greear Ministries, November 6, 2017, https://jdgreear.com/every-worship-leader-wishes-pastor-knew.

Peoples, Katarzyna. *How to Write a Phenomenological Dissertation: A Step-by-Step Guide*. Thousand Oaks: Sage, 2021.

Peretski, Jurgen, and Stacey Peretski, directors. *What God Hath Wrought: Chuck Smith, The Father of the Jesus Movement*. Screen Savers Entertainment (2012). 105 minutes. DVD.

Perez, Adam. "Beyond the Guitar: The Keyboard as a Lens into the History of Contemporary Praise and Worship." *The Hymn* 70.2 (2019) 18–26. https://www.proquest.com/docview/2289418048/fulltextPDF/DB947B54044A41CDPQ.

Pippert, Rebecca Manley. *Out of the Saltshaker and Into the World: Evangelism As a Way of Life*. Downers Grove: InterVarsity, 2021.

Redman, Rob. *The Great Worship Awakening: Singing a new Song in the Postmodern Church*. San Francisco: Jossey Bass.

Reeves, Ryan. "Pentecostalism" Video Lecture (August 10, 2015). YouTube video, 33:24. https://www.youtube.com/watch?v=LzT3pRu2FkY.

Riches, Tanya and Thomas Wagner. *The Hillsong Movement Examined: You Call Me Out upon the Waters*. Cham: Palgrave Macmillan, 2017.

Bibliography

Rozier, Andy. "The Worship Leader and His Pastor." In *Doxology and Theology: How the Gospel Forms the Worship Leader,* edited by Matt Boswell, 141–152. Nashville: Broadman and Holman, 2013.

Sandler, Lauren. *Righteous: Dispatches from the Evangelical Youth Movement.* New York: Viking, 2006.

Schaeffer, Francis A. *Francis Schaeffer Trilogy: The God Who Is There: Escape from Reason: He Is There, and He Is Not Silent.* Westchester: Crossway Books, 1990.

Scott, Jeremy. *Women Who Dared: To Break All the Rules.* La Vergne: Oneworld, 2019.

Sisario, Ben. "Denny Doherty, 66, Mamas and Papas Singer, Dies." *New York Times* (January 20, 2007). https://www.nytimes.com/2007/01/20/arts/music/20doherty.html.

Smith, Chuck. *Calvary Chapel Distinctives.* Costa Mesa: The Word For Today, 2000.

———. *Calvinism, Arminianism & The Word of God.* Costa Mesa: The Word For Today, 2011.

———. *Chuck Smith: A Memoir of Grace.* Edited by Shannon Woodward. Costa Mesa: The Word For Today, 2009.

———. *Living Water: The Power of The Holy Spirit in Your Life.* Costa Mesa: The Word For Today, 2001.

———. *Study Notes for The Word for Today Bible. NKJV.* Costa Mesa: The Word For Today, 2001.

Smith, Chuck, and Brian C. Nixon. *Line Upon Line: Resources for Expounding Upon God's Truth.* Santa Ana: Calvary Chapel Outreach Fellowship, 2007.

Smith, Chuck, and Tal Brooke. *Harvest.* Old Tappan: Fleming H. Revell, 1987.

Smith, Chuck, Jr. *The End of the World as We Know It.* Colorado Springs: Waterbrook, 2001.

Smith, Paul. *New Evangelicalism: The New World Order.* Costa Mesa: The Word For Today, 2011.

Stetzer, Ed. "Thoughts on the Amazing Life of Chuck Smith." Pastors.com (October 3, 2013). https://pastors.com/thoughts-on-the-amazing-life-of-chuck-smith.

Sutton, Matthew Avery. *Aimee Semple McPherson and the Resurrection of Christian America.* Cambridge: Harvard University Press, 2007.

Synan, Vinson and Thomas Nelson. *The Century of the Holy Spirit: 100 Years of Pentecostal and Charismatic Renewal, 1901–2001.* Nashville: Thomas Nelson, 2001.

Thiessen, Henry C. *Lectures in Systematic Theology.* Revised by Vernon D. Doerksen, Grand Rapids: Wm. B. Eerdmans, 1989.

Towns, Elmer L., and Vernon M. Whaley. *Worship Through the Ages: How The Great Awakenings Shape Evangelical Worship.* Nashville: B&H, 2012.

Vaters, Karl. "Pastors And Worship Leaders: 3 Ways To Work Together And 2 Traps To Avoid." *Christianity Today* (June 26, 2019). https://www.christianitytoday.com/karl-vaters/2019/june/pastors-and-worship-leaders.html.

Bibliography

Wahl, Brian. "Your Most Important Relationship as a Worship Leader." Worship Tutorials (September 27, 2017). https://worshiptutorials.com/blog/your-most-important-relationship-as-a-worship-leader.

Ward, Ed. "The Monterey Pop Festival." Encyclopedia Britannica, September 28, 2023. https://www.britannica.com/topic/The-Monterey-Pop-Festival-1688427.

Watts, Simon. "The Beatles and All You Need is Love." BBC. https://www.bbc.co.uk/programmes/p056c8ks.

Weather Underground. "San Bruno (San Francisco), CA Weather History." https://www.wunderground.com/history/daily/KSFO/date/1967-1-14.

Whaley, Vernon M. *Exalt His Name: Understanding Music and Worship, Book* 2. Calumet City: Evangelical Training Association, 2019.

Wilkinson, Michael. "Pentecostalism, the Body, and Embodiment." In *Annual Review of the Sociology of Religion* 8, edited by Michael Wilkinson, and Peter Althouse, 15–35. Leiden: Brill, 2017.

Wimber, John, and Kevin Springer. *Power Evangelism.* Grand Rapids: Chosen Books, 2014.

Wolfgang's Documentaries & Interviews. "Human Be-In." Full Program, 01/14/1967 Polo Fields, Golden Gate Park (Official) (September 25, 2014). https://www.youtube.com/watch?v=HTGyFgyB5Q8.

Yong, Amos. *The Spirit Poured Out on All Flesh: Pentecostalism and the Possibility of Global Theology.* Grand Rapids: Baker Academic. 2005.

Youth for Christ. "Reaching People Everywhere Since 1944." Youth for Christ USA (2021). https://yfc.net/about/history/.

Zuck, Roy B. *Basic Bible Interpretation: A Practical Guide to Discovering Biblical Truth.* Colorado Springs: David C. Cook, 1991.

Subject Index

Afterglow, 23

Believer's Meetings, 23
Baptists, 18
Beatles (The), 48
Biblical Worldview as a lens, 39, 56, 66, 68
Bible as Epistemological Foundation, 7, 35, 67, 92, 110
Bible Reading Plan, 80
Born-Again, 9, 15, 39, 49, 54, 55, 79, 82, 91, 95, 100, 109, 113

California Dreamin', 46
Calling, 35, 78, 101
Calvary Chapel, 53, 86, 95, 99, 118
   Chino Valley, 119
   Costa Mesa, x, xiii, 2, 7, 14, 16, 23, 34, 41, 44, 51, 53, 77, 95
   San Clemente, 64, 92
   Vista, 119
   Yorba Linda, 92
Calvary Chapel Association (CCA), 5
Calvary Global Network (CGN), 5
Charism(a/s), (Charismata), 12, 21, 70, 92, 94, 115
Charismatic, 7, 15, 17, 21, 33, 87, 104, 116
Charismatic (Neo), 8, 24

Charismatic Interpreter, 77, 81, 84, 90, 92, 96, 99, 104, 107, 109, 112, 116
Charismatic Renewal, 19, 24
Church Planters, 4, 6, 34
Commercial Worship Music, 48, 95
Community Rituals, 38, 84, 114
Contemporary Christian Music, xi, 2, 53, 100, 111

Deacon, 81, 112
Doherty, "Papa" Denny, 49

Ecclesia, 22, 49
Educative Process, 102
Espinoza, Gastón, 15, 17, 19

Foursquare Denomination, 4, 11, 21, 29, 37, 40
Frisbee, Lonnie, 118
Fromm, Chuck/Charles, 12, 35, 58, 62, 84, 92, 94, 96
Fruitful Ministry, 5, 40, 49, 54, 55, 62, 66, 72, 76, 88, 99, 101, 104, 107, 115

Gardner-Fischer, Sharon, 10, 12, 44, 103
Geisler, Norman L., 68, 74
Grudem, Wayne A., 77
Gulliksen, Kenn, 34, 35, 37

Subject Index

Schaeffer, Francis, 67, 68
Semple, Robert, 29
Semple-MacPherson, "Sister"
  Aimee, 11, 26, 28–31
Servant Leadership, 81, 106
Seymour, William J., 28
Smith, "Pastor Chuck," x, xvii, 3, 15,
  29, 45, 52, 66, 76, 98, 118
Smith, Kay, x, 10, 11, 13, 28, 32, 42,
  45, 50, 51, 54, 55
Spiritual Renewal, ix, 3, 7, 10, 30,
  32, 45, 54, 65, 87, 98, 104,
  106
Stetzer Ed, 3
Steward, Stewardship, 5, 61, 104,
  107, 111, 114, 116
Summer of Love, 45, 47, 48

Textual Community, 12, 53, 70,
  77, 84, 86, 92, 99, 103, 109,
  112, 114
Tongues, 19
  Glossolalia, 19–21
  Xenolalia, 19–21, 28, 29

Venture(s) of Faith, 93, 105

Vineyard ("The Vineyard") Church,
  34, 35
Vineyard Denomination, xi, 24,
  33–38, 92, 93, 107
Voice 23, 49, 95

Wagner, Peter C. 8, 34, 37
Waves of Pentecostalism, 7, 26,
  24–44
  First, 3, 7, 10–13, 88
  Fourth, 7, 9, 24, 37–39
  Second, 7, 10, 12, 14, 19, 21,
    24, 30–32, 35, 41, 87, 98,
    104, 110
  Third, 7, 33–37, 39, 92, 107
Wholistic, 39, 67, 76
Wimber, John, 7, 34–39, 92, 107
Worship Leader, xv, 1, 26, 40,
  53–64, 66, 68, 72, 77–88,
  90–92, 94, 96, 99–104, 107,
  110, 114, 119, 121
Worship Wars, 53, 62, 109

Yong, Amos, 24

Zschech, Darlene, 26, 28

Scripture Index